Pasta
in minutes

Exciting Entrées, Salads & Side Dishes

by Mable & Gar Hoffman

FISHER
BOOKS

Publishers: Bill Fisher
                               Helen Fisher
                               Howard Fisher
                               J. McCrary

Editor: Veronica Durie

Cover & Illustrations: David Fischer

Book Production: Paula Peterson

Published by Fisher Books
4239 W. Ina Road, Suite 101
Tucson, Arizona 85741
602-744-6110

**Library of Congress
Cataloging-in-Publication Data**

Hoffman, Mable
     Pasta in minutes: exciting entrées,
salads & side dishes / by Mable & Gar
Hoffman.
        p.   cm.
     Includes index.
     ISBN 1-55561-054-4 : $9.95
     1. Cookery (Pasta)   2. Quick and easy
cookery.   I. Hoffman, Gar.   II. Title.
TX809.M17H58   1993
641.8'22--dc20   93-20767
                                      CIP

Notice: The information in this book is true and
complete to the best of our knowledge. It is
offered with no guarantees on the part of the
authors or Fisher Books. The authors and
publisher disclaim all liability in connection with
use of this book.

Contents

About the Authors

Mable and Gar Hoffman are among the world's bestselling cookbook authors. Five of their cookbooks have won the *R. T. French Tastemaker Award*, the "Oscar" for cookbooks. Their first cookbook, *Crockery Cookery*, was a very successful collaboration with the Fishers. Their joint effort resulted in a bestseller on the *New York Times* list for a record number of weeks. More than 18 years later, the book remains popular and still enjoys widespread appeal. Because crockery cooking is still extremely popular, the Hoffmans worked with Fisher Books in creating a companion book, *Crockery Favorites*. Other Fisher Books authored by the Hoffmans include *Cookies in Minutes, Frozen Yogurt, Ice Cream* and *Carefree Entertaining*.

The Hoffmans own and manage Hoffman Food Consultants, Inc. In addition to writing cookbooks, Mable has served as a consultant to many national food companies and publications.

Mable and Gar concentrate their efforts on food styling, recipe development and writing. They travel worldwide gathering ideas and keeping abreast of food trends and ethnic cuisines.

Acknowledgements

The Hoffmans extend a special thanks to Jan Robertson for her invaluable assistance in recipe development and testing for *Pasta in Minutes*.

Pasta in Minutes

Pasta is a favorite with people of all ages and nationalities. It plays an important role in our culinary lives from our first childhood taste of spaghetti or noodle casserole to the most elegant pasta presentations enjoyed in the finest restaurants.

Gone are the days when the image of pasta was limited to dishes overflowing with tomato sauces. Now we combine it with an unbelievable variety of foods, including fresh vegetables, cheeses from around the world, exotic sauces, and a never-ending assortment of popular convenience foods.

Busy cooks choose pasta so they can put dinner on the table within a few minutes. The topping can be as simple as fresh herbs and cheese, or selected from a cornucopia of ethnic and regional foods. Basic pasta serves as the ideal base for flavorful combinations of sauces, toppings and fillings. And what's wonderful is—pasta is *good* for you!

Many recipes in ***Pasta in Minutes*** are versatile and may be used as appetizers, salads or main dishes, depending on the quantities you serve. Recipes will make about four servings if pasta is your entrée; about six salad servings; and probably eight to ten appetizers, first courses or starters.

It is not necessary to use the exact shape of pasta indicated in our recipes. In most cases, we suggest two kinds for you to consider. If your favorites are not listed, and they are similar to our selections, we encourage you to use them.

Types of Pasta

There's a wide choice of pasta to use in your favorite dishes. Your selection will depend on the amount of time you are willing to spend, the total cost of the dish, and your preferences regarding specific flavors or textures.

Dry uncooked pasta—available in many shapes and sold in all grocery stores. Popular shapes include elbow macaroni, spaghetti and lasagne noodles.

Refrigerated pasta—traditional fettucine and tortellini as well as other pastas are found in the deli or cheese section of super-markets, gourmet shops, pasta shops and delicatessens. Must be refrigerated until preparation time. Directions are on individual packages.

Frozen pasta—found in freezer sections of most grocery stores and also available in some gourmet stores and pasta shops.

Fresh pasta—available in pasta shops or you can make your own, page 11.

Dry cooked pasta—crisp noodles used for topping soups or as a base for salads and main dishes.

Oriental influences—won-ton or egg-roll wrappers, rice sticks and cellophane noodles used for appetizers, main dishes and soups; available in supermarkets and Asian food stores.

How to choose pasta shapes

While some regions have different traditions, there are some basic rules for matching pastas with their sauces or toppings.

Fine, delicate pastas should be paired with light sauces and small ingredients.

Long, thin pasta takes a sauce that clings.

Flat, wide pasta (noodles) work well with rich sauces.

Twisted and hollow pasta can be matched with chunky sauces.

Popular Pasta Shapes

Most commercial pasta is made from durum wheat. When pasta is colored green, red, orange or yellow, it is flavored and colored by the addition of spinach, herb, beet, tomato or saffron. The pasta we tested for this book is listed below by basic shape. Some names vary with the area of the world where they originated or with the individual manufacturer.

mostaccioli
(ridged and plain tubes)

medium egg noodles

radiatore
(little radiators)

rotelles
(wagon wheels)

cavatappi
(spiral macaroni)

medium shells

penne
(quill macaroni)

corkscrews
(spirals)

Small shapes

alphabets

small shells

fine egg noodles

stars

orzo

tripolini
(very small bow ties)

salad macaroni
(rings)

Medium shapes

elbow macaroni

spaghetti twists

ziti

gnocchi
(shells)

cavatelli
(narrow, ripple-edged shells)

Large shapes

rigatoni
(large grooved macaroni)

medium-large bow-ties
(with rounded edges)

large bow-ties
(with square edges)

large elbow macaroni

occhi di lupo
(large tube)

large shells

Extra-large shapes

lasagne

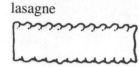

manicotti

jumbo shells

Long shapes

spaghetti

fettucine

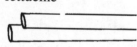

capellini
(angel hair)

traditional fusilli
(long twists)

spaghettini

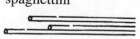

linguine

perciatelli
(hollow spaghetti)

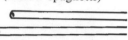

bean threads
(cellophane noodles)

Filled pastas

ravioli

agnolotti

capelletti

tortellini
(small)

tortelloni
(large)

Cooking Pasta
Secrets to Success

A large deep pan. You may call it a *spaghetti cooker, stock pot, Dutch Oven* or a variety of other names. We like the six- or eight-quart size for cooking pasta. Our favorite model has a removable liner similar to a colander. The liner has perforations around the side and bottom for the boiling water to circulate while cooking. The liner can be lifted out for easy draining when the pasta is done. If your favorite pan does not have a liner similar to ours, drain the cooked pasta in a colander or large strainer.

Boiling water. It is important to bring water to a full rolling boil before adding any pasta. When adding long strands of pasta such as spaghetti, hold one end of a small bunch of it, and gently lower the other end into rolling boiling water. The rolling motion of the water keeps the pasta moving around, resulting in more even cooking and less sticking together.

Check for desired doneness. Cooking times vary with the size and shape of pasta. Look for package directions regarding cooking times. One or two minutes before the cooking time indicated on the package, remove one or two strands or pieces of pasta from the boiling water. Cover with cold water to cool, then taste it. If it is the texture you prefer, remove the pan from the heat and drain. If it is too firm for your taste, continue cooking another minute or two and check again. Total time will depend on your individual preference. Some people enjoy pasta when it is *al dente* or fairly firm; others prefer it softer and more pliable. Remember fresh pasta cooks much faster than packaged dry varieties.

Draining pasta. If you cook pasta in a pan with a removable liner, lift the liner to drain the pasta into the pan or sink. Discard the water. Without a perforated liner, pour cooked pasta into a colander or large strainer; drain well. Water left on cooked pasta will dilute the sauce, making it too thin, resulting in a less flavorful dish.

Rinsing cooked pasta. This process varies with individual recipes, methods and ways of preparing pasta. In most recipes for hot pasta dishes, we drained, then quickly rinsed with hot water. Rinsing cooked pasta stops the cooking process, preventing over-cooking. Obviously, some of the starch is rinsed away with this method and sauces may not stick to the pasta quite as well. On the other hand, the flavors of the sauces seem to be more forceful when used with rinsed pasta. For pasta salads, we always rinse the cooked pasta with cold water to cool it before adding other cool ingredients and dressing.

What to cook first. In most recipes, we suggest that you start by heating water for pasta. While it is heating, measure ingredients for sauce or topping. Then make the sauce or topping while the pasta cooks. If it is not practical to combine the sauce with the cooked pasta as soon as it is done, toss the drained cooked pasta with a small amount of oil to prevent it from sticking together.

Salt or no salt. We did not add salt to the water when cooking pasta. If you think that salt is necessary, add one or two teaspoons to the water before adding uncooked pasta.

How much pasta to cook. The amount of pasta is dependent on the way you use it. If a pasta salad or casserole is practically a complete meal, the amount should be much larger than one that is used as an accompaniment to meat, fish or poultry. Most of our

recipes start with eight ounces of pasta; compatible ingredients are added to form a main dish. Most of them will make four to five average servings.

How to estimate amounts of pasta. Most uncooked, dry pasta is available in 16-ounce (one-pound) packages. If you have a kitchen scale, weigh the amount you need for a recipe. If not, don't worry about the exact amount. Just estimate half of the package (eight ounces) and proceed according to directions. A fraction of an ounce over or under the required amount is not critical. However, if you use much more pasta than indicated in the recipe, the dish will be too dry unless you increase the sauce or dressing.

Measurements used for uncooked dry pasta:

Small shapes—number of ounces plus cup measurements for uncooked shapes such as elbow macaroni or spirals.

Long strands—number of ounces for pastas such as fettucine or spaghetti. It is not possible to make cup measurements without breaking uncooked long pasta into small pieces.

Extra large shapes— manicotti and extra-large shells are measured by the unit (for example, 4 manicotti shells).

Making Your Own Fresh Pasta

Most of the recipes in this book were tested with dry pasta because such a wide variety of shapes and sizes is available in markets. Dry pastas are quick and easy to prepare, enabling you to create *pasta in minutes.*

Knowing that everyone loves fresh pasta, we have included our favorite basic recipe. Just follow this recipe, then combine it with a sauce or topping.

Fresh Homemade Pasta
1-1/2 cups all-purpose flour
2 large eggs
2 teaspoons vegetable oil

Make a mound of flour on a clean work surface or in a large bowl. Form a deep well in center. Break eggs into center; add oil. Beat eggs and oil lightly with a fork. Gradually stir in flour from sides of the mound, using a circular motion. When dough becomes stiff, mix with your hands. Form into a ball; knead 5 minutes. Follow directions for pasta machine or with rolling pin, roll into 16- or 17-inch circle by stretching dough from center. Let rest, uncovered, 15 to 20 minutes or until surface begins to look dry. Fold over and over to make a flat roll about 3 inches wide. Cut desired widths. Let dry at least 5 minutes. Drop into boiling water. Cook 1 to 2 minutes or until desired degree of doneness. Makes 3 to 4 servings.

Pasta Meals in Minutes

When time is short and everyone in your family is anxious for a quick dinner, here are some helpful tips and shortcuts to make it easier to present an appetizing pasta meal in minutes.

Fruits and vegetables. Buy fresh vegetables that are trimmed and cut into bite-size pieces.

Look for pre-shredded cabbage and ready-to-serve green-salad combinations.

Complete your quick pasta dinner with cut-up fruits and melons from the deli or super-market refrigerated cases. Add a few fresh strawberries or raspberries, if desired.

Keep a package of combination vegetables in the freezer to add to pasta with a tomato or cream sauce.

Cheese. At the market look for shredded cheese to add to sauces or to sprinkle on cooked pasta.

For a quick dish, toss cooked pasta with crumbled feta or goat cheese and chopped fresh herbs; top with chopped plum tomatoes.

Poultry. Keep cooked chicken or turkey in your freezer for last-minute sauces or toppings on hot pasta dishes or refreshing salads.

Pick up whole barbecued chicken at the market or deli; cut into individual pieces to serve with your favorite pasta.

Meats. Thinly sliced cooked ham, pastrami or salami from the deli are welcome additions to impromptu pasta-salad plates.

For a special brunch, add strips of Canadian bacon or small cocktail sausages to a pasta with a creamy sauce.

Chop leftover roast pork or beef. Sprinkle over cooked pasta; serve with salsa or marinara sauce.

Fish and seafood. Open a can of tuna or salmon; combine with refrigerated pasta.

Keep a package of shelled cooked shrimp in the freezer; thaw and add to a salad or main dish.

Cutting Calories & Fat

Pasta is a food that is high in complex carbohydrates, yet low in fat. The problem is that most of us add sauces and toppings to pasta, creating dishes that are high in fat and calories. If you are a pasta-lover, you'll find these suggestions helpful when trying to lower calories and reduce fat content.

Fresh herbs and garden-fresh vegetables add a lot of flavor to pasta dishes, with practically no increase in calories or fat.

Take advantage of vitamin and flavor-laden sliced red, yellow, orange or green peppers for a welcome addition to pasta sauces. No one will miss a slight reduction of meat or cheese with these colorful surprises.

Substitute half and half in a recipe that traditionally uses whipping cream.

Low-fat or nonfat plain yogurt provides a low-calorie base for pasta sauces. Use it to replace all or part of dairy products with higher fat content.

Family Favorites

To a very young child, the word *pasta* translates as *spaghetti*. Older children usually widen their interest to macaroni and cheese, lasagne and a few noodle dishes.

Busy parents depend on pasta dishes to satisfy growing appetites. Hearty combinations of pasta with poultry or meats and sauces result in stick-to-the-ribs type family recipes such as our version of the ever-popular Tuna Noodle Special.

Skillet Macaroni & Cheese

If Canadian bacon is not available, substitute baked or boiled ham.

8 oz. elbow macaroni or cavatappi (about 2 cups uncooked)
1 (8-oz.) pkg. Neufchâtel cheese, cubed
1-3/4 cups milk
2 tablespoons Dijon-style mustard
1 teaspoon Worcestershire sauce
1/4 teaspoon dried dill
1 (10-oz.) pkg. frozen peas and carrots, cooked, drained
3/4 cup thinly sliced Canadian bacon, chopped (about 3-1/2 oz.)
1 cup shredded Swiss cheese (4 oz.)

Cook pasta according to package directions; drain. Rinse with hot water; drain and set aside. In a large skillet over low heat, stir Neufchâtel, milk, mustard and Worcestershire sauce until smooth. Stir in dill, cooked vegetables, Canadian bacon and drained cooked pasta. Sprinkle with Swiss cheese. Heat until cheese melts. Makes 4 to 6 servings.

Family Favorite Spaghetti Sauce

The ever-popular traditional spaghetti that you can make within 30 minutes.

8 oz. spaghetti
1 lb. lean ground beef
1 medium onion, chopped
1 garlic clove, crushed
1 (28-oz.) can crushed tomatoes
2 (8-oz.) cans tomato sauce
1 teaspoon chopped fresh oregano or
    1/4 teaspoon dried-leaf oregano
2 teaspoons chopped fresh basil or
    1/2 teaspoon dried-leaf basil
1/4 cup dry red wine
2 tablespoons chopped parsley
1/4 teaspoon salt
1/8 teaspoon pepper
Grated Parmesan cheese

Cook pasta according to package directions; drain. Rinse with hot water; drain and set aside in a large warm serving bowl. While pasta cooks, combine beef, onion and garlic in a 3-or 4-quart pan; cook and stir 3 or 4 minutes. Add crushed tomatoes, tomato sauce, oregano, basil, wine, parsley, salt and pepper. Cover and simmer 15 minutes. Spoon over drained cooked pasta. Sprinkle with Parmesan cheese. Makes 5 or 6 servings.

Deluxe Macaroni & Cheese

Our favorite macaroni and cheese; made with processed and natural cheeses for the best flavor and texture.

8 oz. elbow macaroni or spirals (2-1/4 to 2-1/2 cups uncooked)
2 tablespoons margarine or butter
2 tablespoons all-purpose flour
3 cups milk
1/2 teaspoon seasoned salt
1/8 teaspoon pepper
1/4 teaspoon paprika
1 teaspoon dry mustard
2 cups shredded sharp process cheese (8 oz.)
2 cups shredded sharp Cheddar cheese (8 oz.)

Cook pasta according to package directions; drain. Rinse with hot water; drain and set aside. Preheat oven to 375F (190C). While pasta cooks, melt margarine or butter in a 2- or 3-quart saucepan. Stir in flour; heat until bubbly. Gradually add milk; heat and stir until slightly thickened. Add drained cooked pasta and remaining ingredients except 1 cup Cheddar cheese. Spoon into an 11" x 8" or 2-1/2-quart baking dish. Sprinkle top with remaining cheese. Bake in preheated oven about 25 minutes or until bubbly.
Makes 6 or 7 servings.

All-American Lasagne

Bacon, cheese and tomatoes create a pasta dish that is as delicious as the popular sandwich made with that combination.

8 oz. lasagne noodles
1/4 cup margarine or butter
1/4 cup all-purpose flour
1/4 teaspoon salt
1/8 teaspoon pepper
1-1/2 teaspoons prepared mustard
3-1/2 cups milk
8 slices bacon, cooked, drained, crumbled
3 medium tomatoes, thinly sliced
3 green onions, thinly sliced
2 cups shredded Cheddar or American cheese (8 oz.)

Cook pasta according to package directions; drain. Rinse with hot water; drain and set aside. In a medium saucepan, melt margarine or butter; stir in flour, salt, pepper and mustard. Gradually add milk; heat and stir until bubbly and thickened. In a 13" x 9" baking pan, arrange alternate layers of drained cooked pasta, sauce, bacon, sliced tomatoes and green onions. Repeat layering. Top with shredded cheese. Preheat oven to 350F (175C). Bake in preheated oven 35 to 45 minutes or until bubbly. Makes 4 to 6 servings.

Tuna Noodle Special

An updated lower-calorie version of a traditional childhood favorite.

8 oz. fusilli or twists (about 3-1/4 cups uncooked)
1 tablespoon vegetable oil
1 small onion, chopped
1 cup sliced mushrooms (2 to 3 oz.)
3 tablespoons all-purpose flour
1 (14-1/2-oz.) can chicken broth
1 (12-oz.) can evaporated skimmed milk
1/4 teaspoon salt
1/8 teaspoon pepper
1 (12-oz.) can chunk light tuna packed in water, drained,
**   flaked**
1/2 cup grated Cheddar cheese, if desired

Cook pasta according to package directions; drain, rinse with hot water; drain and set aside. While pasta cooks, heat oil in a 10-inch skillet. Add onion and mushrooms; cook and stir 1 minute. Add flour, then chicken broth, evaporated milk, salt, pepper and tuna. Cook over medium heat until bubbly. Stir in drained cooked pasta. Sprinkle with cheese, if desired. Makes 4 to 6 servings.

Sausage & Mushroom Pizza Pie

The pizza pan will be quite full. Use the minimum amount of pasta if your pan does not have a rim to contain the mixture.

6 to 8 oz. angel hair or vermicelli
1 tablespoon vegetable oil
1/2 cup sliced mushrooms
4 oz. smoked sausage, thinly sliced (about 3/4 cup)
1 small green or yellow bell pepper, seeded, thinly sliced
2 green onions, sliced
1 (14-oz.) jar pizza sauce
1 cup shredded mozzarella cheese (4 oz.)

Cook pasta according to package directions; drain. Rinse; drain again and toss with oil in a large bowl. Press on the bottom of a 12-inch pizza pan. Preheat oven to 400F (205C). Top cooked pasta with mushrooms, smoked sausage, bell pepper and green onions. Pour pizza sauce over all. Sprinkle with cheese. Bake in preheated oven 15 to 20 minutes or until cheese melts. Cut into wedges.

Makes about 6 servings.

Chicken & Noodles

If your family prefers thighs or drumsticks, buy about two pounds; remove skin and bones before dicing and cooking.

8 oz. medium noodles
2 tablespoons margarine or butter
1 lb. boneless skinless chicken breasts, diced
2 tablespoons all-purpose flour
1 (14-1/2-oz.) can chicken broth
2 green onions, chopped
2 tablespoons dry white wine
1/2 teaspoon salt
1/8 teaspoon pepper
1/2 cup dairy sour cream

Cook pasta according to package directions; drain. Rinse with hot water; drain and set aside. While pasta cooks, heat margarine or butter in a large skillet. Add chicken. Cook and stir 3 or 4 minutes. Stir in flour; then chicken broth, green onions, wine, salt and pepper. Cook over low heat until slightly thickened. Remove from heat. Stir in sour cream, then drained cooked noodles. Makes 4 to 6 servings.

Home-Style Make-Ahead Short Ribs with Fettucine

Bake the ribs ahead of time and refrigerate. Then cook pasta and reheat ribs just before serving.

3 to 4 lbs. beef short ribs
1 (14-1/2-oz.) can condensed beef broth
2 tablespoons Worcestershire sauce
2 tablespoons catsup
1/4 cup dry red wine
1/2 teaspoon salt
1/8 teaspoon pepper
1 small onion, chopped
3 tablespoons cornstarch
1/4 cup cold water
8 oz. fettucine or noodles

Preheat oven to 325F (165C). Place ribs in a 13" x 9" baking pan. In a small bowl, combine broth, Worcestershire sauce, catsup, wine, salt, pepper and onion. Pour over meat. Cover; bake in preheated oven 2 hours or until very tender. Refrigerate overnight or several hours. Using a large spoon or spatula, remove fat from top of sauce. In a cup, dissolve cornstarch in cold water. Add to sauce and meat. Heat and stir until thickened. Meanwhile, cook pasta according to package directions; drain and set aside in a large warm serving bowl. Arrange meat and sauce on drained cooked pasta. Makes 4 to 6 servings.

Imperial Macaroni Bake

It's easier to serve if you let the finished dish stand about 10 minutes before cutting.

**6 oz. small elbow macaroni or mini-bow pasta
     (about 1-1/2 cups uncooked)**
12 oz. pork sausage
4 eggs, beaten slightly
3 cups milk
2 tablespoons chopped pimento
1/2 teaspoon dry mustard
2 tablespoons finely chopped fresh basil
2 cups shredded mozzarella cheese (8 oz.)
1/4 teaspoon salt
1/8 teaspoon pepper
1/4 cup grated Parmesan or Romano cheese

Cook pasta according to package directions; drain. Rinse with hot water; drain and set aside. While pasta cooks, brown sausage in a small skillet; drain. In a large bowl, combine eggs, milk, drained cooked pasta, cooked sausage, pimento, mustard, basil, mozzarella cheese, salt and pepper. Preheat oven to 350F (175C). Spoon mixture into a 13" x 9" baking dish. Sprinkle with Parmesan or Romano cheese. Bake in preheated oven about 55 minutes or until firm. Makes 5 or 6 servings.

Many-Layered Ricotta-Vegetable Bake

*Small pasta shells enhanced by spaghetti sauce and fresh
vegetables—with a Cheddar-cheese topping.*

8 oz. small shells or tripolini (about 2-1/4 cups uncooked)
2 tablespoons vegetable oil
2 medium peeled carrots, shredded
2 medium zucchini, shredded
2 green onions, finely chopped
1/2 teaspoon salt
1/8 teaspoon pepper
1 garlic clove, crushed
2 eggs, beaten slightly
1 cup ricotta cheese (8 oz.)
1 (28-oz.) jar spaghetti sauce
1 cup shredded Cheddar cheese (4 oz.)

Cook pasta according to package directions; drain. Rinse
with hot water; drain and set aside. While pasta cooks, heat
oil in a large skillet. Add carrots, zucchini, green onions,
salt, pepper and garlic. Cook and stir several minutes or until
vegetables are soft. Spread half the vegetables on the bottom
of a 2-quart baking dish. Top with drained cooked pasta. In a
small bowl, combine beaten eggs and ricotta. Spoon over
pasta. Top with remaining vegetables, then spaghetti sauce.
Sprinkle with cheese. Preheat oven to 375F (190C). Bake
about 40 minutes or until bubbly. Makes 4 to 6 servings.

Dilled Sour-Cream
Salmon-with-Spinach Fettucine

Flavor and color of spinach fettucine make an exciting contrast to creamy salmon sauce.

8 oz. spinach or regular fettucine
8 oz. fresh boned skinned salmon, cubed
1/2 cup dry white wine
3 green onions, sliced
2 tablespoons chopped fresh dill
1 tablespoon cornstarch
1/4 teaspoon salt
1/8 teaspoon seasoned salt
1/8 teaspoon pepper
1 cup dairy sour cream
Fresh dill sprigs, coarsely chopped

Cook pasta according to package directions; drain. Rinse with hot water; drain and set aside in a large warm serving bowl. While pasta cooks, combine salmon, wine, green onions, dill, cornstarch, salt, seasoned salt and pepper in a 2-quart saucepan. Cook and stir over medium heat until slightly thickened. Add sour cream. Stir over low heat until hot. Spoon over drained cooked pasta; toss until well blended. Garnish with additional sprigs of dill.
Makes 4 to 6 servings.

On-the-Go Breakfast Roll-Ups

Timesaving savory roll-ups that you can pick up and eat on-the-go.

3 hard-cooked eggs, chopped
1/3 cup finely chopped cooked ham
1 teaspoon minced green onion
1/2 teaspoon Dijon-style mustard
1 tablespoon finely chopped chutney
2 tablespoons plain low-fat yogurt
1/4 teaspoon curry powder
4 egg-roll skins (6 inches square)
1/4 cup vegetable oil

In a medium bowl, combine hard-cooked eggs, ham, green onion, mustard, chutney, yogurt and curry powder. Spoon about 3 tablespoons on center of each egg-roll skin. Fold over ends, then roll up. Moisten ends with water to seal.

Heat oil in an 8-inch skillet. Brown roll-ups on both sides. Makes 4 roll-ups.

Versatile Pasta Salads

There's a pasta salad to suit every occasion and all seasons. In the summertime, gardens and roadside stands offer a bountiful array of fresh fruits and vegetables to enhance these salads. For a healthy choice, try Asparagus-Prosciutto Pasta Bowl. Refreshing slices of honeydew and cantaloupe make tasty edible containers for fresh summer fruits and pasta salads.

Toppings and dressings for pasta salads range from reduced-calorie mayonnaise to a quick-and-easy combination of balsamic vinegar and olive oil. Others create an Oriental accent with a touch of hoisin sauce or sesame oil.

Scalini Artichoke Salad

For a special touch, sprinkle with grated Romano cheese.

8 oz. penne or fusilli (about 3 cups uncooked)
1 (6-oz.) jar marinated artichoke hearts, drained, sliced
1 small red or yellow bell pepper, chopped
1 tablespoon chopped chives
1/4 cup olive oil
2 tablespoons balsamic vinegar
1/4 teaspoon salt
1/8 teaspoon pepper
4 oz. salami, cut into thin strips

Cook pasta according to package directions; drain. Rinse with cold water; drain and cool. In a large serving bowl, combine sliced artichoke hearts, bell pepper, chives, olive oil, vinegar, salt and pepper. Add drained cooked pasta and salami. Toss until well-blended. Makes 4 to 6 servings.

Tropic Breeze Salad

Bean-thread noodles are transparent and sometimes called cellophane noodles.

4 oz. bean-thread noodles
1 lb. lean ground pork
1 teaspoon finely chopped fresh ginger
1 garlic clove, crushed
1/8 teaspoon red-pepper flakes
3 green onions, sliced
1 ripe mango, peeled, diced
2 tablespoons hoisin sauce
1 tablespoon sesame oil
1/4 cup soy sauce

In a large bowl, pour boiling water over noodles and let stand 20 minutes; drain. Rinse with hot water; drain and set aside. In a large skillet, lightly brown pork over medium heat; drain off fat. Add ginger, garlic, red-pepper flakes and green onions to skillet. Cook and stir 2 or 3 minutes. Add well-drained noodles, mango, hoisin sauce, sesame oil and soy sauce. Toss until well-blended. Serve warm or refrigerate several hours and serve chilled.
Makes 4 to 6 servings.

Hot Bacon Pasta Salad

An impressive dish to serve at a backyard barbecue or take to a potluck get-together.

8 oz. pasta spirals or rotini (2-1/4 to 2-1/2 cups uncooked)
4 bacon slices, diced
3 tablespoons sugar
1 tablespoon cornstarch
1/3 cup white wine
1/4 teaspoon salt
1/8 teaspoon black pepper
3/4 cup chicken bouillon or broth
2 medium pattypan squash or zucchini, shredded, drained
1/4 cup chopped red onion
1 medium peeled carrot, shredded

Cook pasta according to package directions; drain. Rinse with cold water; drain and set aside. Cook bacon in a large skillet. Drain, leaving 2 tablespoons drippings and cooked bacon in skillet. Stir in sugar, cornstarch, wine, salt, pepper and bouillon or broth. Cook and stir over medium heat until slightly thickened. In a large serving bowl, combine drained cooked pasta, uncooked squash, onion, carrot and hot bacon sauce. Toss until well-blended. Serve at room temperature or chill 2 hours. Makes 4 to 6 servings.

Midsummer Honeydew-Turkey Plates

Cook and cool turkey and pasta ahead of time so they'll be ready to combine with the other ingredients.

8 oz. medium bow ties or medium shells (3-1/2 to 4 cups)
1 medium honeydew melon
6 large lettuce leaves
2 cups seedless red grapes
2 cups cooled, diced, cooked turkey
1 cup low-fat orange yogurt
1/2 teaspoon grated orange peel
2 teaspoons finely chopped crystallized ginger
1 teaspoon curry powder
1/4 cup chopped toasted almonds

Cook pasta according to package directions; drain. Rinse with cold water; drain and cool. Peel melon. Cut into 6 thin crosswise slices; remove seeds. Cube remaining end pieces of melon. Arrange lettuce leaves on 6 individual plates. Top each with a ring of melon. In a large bowl, combine remaining melon cubes, grapes, turkey and cooled cooked pasta. Add yogurt, orange peel, ginger and curry powder. Toss; serve in melon rings on lettuce. Sprinkle with almonds. Makes 6 generous luncheon servings.

Sicilian Salad

A satisfying, hearty salad that's an ideal summertime main dish.

8 oz. cavatelli or medium shells (about 2-1/2 cups uncooked)
1 (6-oz.) jar marinated artichoke hearts, drained, quartered
20 to 24 slices pepperoni, halved (about 2 oz.)
1/2 cup sliced black olives
1 cup ricotta cheese (8 oz.)
1/2 cup Italian salad dressing
2 tablespoons grated Romano or Parmesan cheese

Cook pasta according to package directions; drain. Rinse with cold water; drain and refrigerate. In a large serving bowl, combine artichoke hearts, pepperoni, olives, ricotta cheese, salad dressing and cooled cooked pasta. Toss until well-blended. Sprinkle top with Romano cheese.
Makes 4 main dishes or 8 side salads.

California Club Salad

Fresh oranges and avocados enhance a flavorful smoked turkey-and-cheese salad.

8 oz. ziti or corkscrews (3 to 3-1/2 cups uncooked)
2 oranges, peeled, cut in chunks
1 avocado, peeled, diced
1 (6-oz.) jar marinated artichoke hearts, drained
4 to 5 oz. smoked turkey, cut into thin strips (about 1 cup)
4 oz. Monterey Jack cheese, cut into thin strips (about 1 cup)
1/2 cup sliced ripe olives

Dressing:
1/4 cup raspberry vinegar
1/2 cup olive oil or vegetable oil
1/4 teaspoon salt
1/2 teaspoon chili powder

Cook pasta according to package directions; drain. Rinse with cold water; drain and cool. In a large bowl, combine orange chunks, diced avocados, artichoke hearts, smoked turkey, cheese and drained cooked pasta. Pour dressing over all; toss. Sprinkle with olives. Makes 4 to 6 servings.

Dressing:
Combine ingredients in a small bowl.

Niçoise Pasta Platter

A main-dish salad plate for those who like nutritious meals that are good to eat.

**8 oz. medium shells or elbow macaroni
(about 2-1/2 cups uncooked)**
1 (6-oz.) can light tuna in water, drained, flaked
2 hard-cooked eggs, sliced
1 small red onion, sliced
1/2 cup sliced black olives
1-1/2 to 2 cups cooked green beans, cut into 1-inch pieces
1/3 cup olive oil
3 tablespoons lemon juice
1 teaspoon chopped fresh oregano
1 tablespoon capers, drained
1/2 teaspoon salt
1/8 teaspoon pepper
2 fresh Italian plum tomatoes, cut into thin wedges

Cook pasta according to package directions; drain. Rinse with cold water; drain. In a shallow serving bowl, combine drained cooked pasta, tuna, eggs, onion, olives and green beans. Add olive oil, lemon juice, oregano, capers, salt and pepper. Toss until well-blended. Arrange tomato wedges on top. Makes 4 to 6 servings.

Dreams-of-the-Orient Salad

Chow-mein noodles add a welcome crunchy topping to this salad.

1/4 cup vegetable oil
2 tablespoons white-wine vinegar
1 garlic clove, crushed
1 teaspoon honey
1 tablespoon soy sauce
2 teaspoons sesame oil
2 cups diced cooked turkey or chicken
1/2 cup sliced canned water chestnuts
1 papaya or mango, peeled, diced
1/2 cup Chinese pea pods
1 small head Boston or Bibb lettuce
1 to 1-1/4 cups Chinese chow-mein noodles

In a measuring cup or small bowl, combine oil, vinegar, garlic, honey, soy sauce and sesame oil. In a large bowl, combine turkey or chicken, water chestnuts, papaya or mango and pea pods. Add oil mixture; toss until well-blended. Arrange lettuce leaves on individual plates. Add turkey mixture; sprinkle chow-mein noodles over all. Makes 4 or 5 servings.

Curried Pasta Stars in Tomato Shells

Line your prettiest salad plates with leafy green lettuce; add a tomato with curried stars for an impressive luncheon dish.

4 oz. miniature pasta stars or shells (about 3/4 cup uncooked)
3 hard-cooked eggs, chopped
1/3 cup reduced-calorie mayonnaise
1/2 teaspoon curry powder
1/4 teaspoon salt
1 teaspoon Dijon-style mustard
4 thin slices Canadian bacon, julienned
5 large tomatoes
2 teaspoons finely chopped fresh basil

Cook pasta according to package directions; drain. Rinse with cold water; drain. In a medium bowl, combine hard-cooked eggs, mayonnaise, drained cooked pasta, curry powder, salt, mustard and Canadian bacon. Slice top off each tomato; scoop out pulp with a spoon. Discard juice and most of seeds. Chop pulp; add to egg mixture. Spoon into tomato shells. Sprinkle with chopped basil. Makes 5 servings.

Ham & Egg Salad Twist

A popular dish for a Sunday brunch or luncheon buffet.

8 oz. corkscrews or rotini (2-1/2 to 3 cups uncooked)
1 cup diced ham or diced cooked turkey
3 hard-cooked eggs, coarsely chopped
1/4 cup chopped red or green bell pepper
1/2 cup reduced-calorie mayonnaise
2 tablespoons milk
2 teaspoons Dijon-style mustard
1 teaspoon sugar
2 teaspoons vinegar
1/4 teaspoon salt
1/8 teaspoon pepper
2 tablespoons chopped chives

Cook pasta according to package directions; drain. Rinse
with cold water; drain and set aside or refrigerate in a large
serving bowl. When cooked pasta is cool, add ham, eggs and
bell pepper. In a small bowl, combine mayonnaise, milk,
mustard, sugar, vinegar, salt and pepper. Stir into pasta
mixture. Sprinkle with chopped chives. Refrigerate until
serving time. Makes 4 or 5 servings.

Tri-Color Pepper Pasta

For a make-ahead salad, combine all ingredients except pasta; refrigerate several hours. Add cooked cooled pasta at the last minute.

**5 to 6 oz. spiral twists or corkscrews
    (1-3/4 to 2 cups uncooked)**
1/3 cup vegetable oil
1 medium yellow or orange bell pepper, cut into thin strips
1 small cucumber, coarsely shredded
1 small red onion, sliced
1/4 cup dry white wine
1/2 teaspoon salt
1/8 teaspoon pepper
2 tablespoons chopped fresh dill
1 tablespoon chopped chives
1 tomato, cut in chunks

Cook pasta according to package directions; drain. Rinse with cold water; drain. In a large salad bowl, combine drained cooked pasta, oil, bell-pepper strips, shredded cucumber, sliced onion, wine, salt, pepper, fresh dill and chives. Toss until well-blended. Top with tomato chunks. Makes 4 or 5 servings.

Adriatic Tuna Toss

For an interesting presentation, garnish the salad bowl with sliced hard-cooked eggs and slivers of dill pickle.

8 oz. cavatappi or corkscrews (3-1/4 cups uncooked)
1 (6-1/4-oz.) can water-packed tuna, well-drained, flaked
1/2 cup mayonnaise
2 tablespoons lemon juice
1 teaspoon dry mustard
1/8 teaspoon red-pepper flakes
1/4 cup finely chopped celery
2 tablespoons finely chopped parsley
1 tablespoon finely chopped chives
1 tablespoon capers, drained
2 tablespoons sliced ripe olives, if desired

Cook pasta according to package directions; drain. Rinse with cold water; drain and set aside. While pasta cooks, combine tuna, mayonnaise, lemon juice, mustard and red-pepper flakes in a blender or food processor; blend until almost smooth. Stir in celery, parsley, chives and capers. In a large serving bowl, spoon sauce over cooled drained pasta. Toss until well-blended. Garnish with sliced olives, if desired. Makes 4 to 6 servings.

Taste-of-the-Orient Salad Bowl

An impressive, yet nutritious luncheon salad with Oriental flavors.

8 oz. ziti or rigatoni (3 cups uncooked)
2 cups chopped cooked turkey or chicken
1 cup sliced mushrooms (about 6 medium)
1 cup Chinese pea pods, halved (about 3 oz.)
1 mango, peeled, cubed
2 green onions, sliced
1 carrot, peeled, shredded
1/2 cup vegetable oil
3 tablespoons white-wine vinegar
1 to 2 teaspoons grated fresh ginger
1 tablespoons soy sauce
1 tablespoon toasted sesame seeds

Cook pasta according to package directions; drain. Rinse with cold water; drain and cool. In a large serving bowl, combine cooled cooked pasta, turkey or chicken, mushrooms, pea pods, mango, green onions and carrot. In a small bowl, combine oil, vinegar, ginger and soy sauce. Pour over pasta mixture; toss to blend. Sprinkle with sesame seeds. Makes 4 or 5 servings.

Asparagus-Prosciutto Pasta Bowl

*In a hurry? Substitute a 10-ounce package of
frozen asparagus.*

8 oz. cavatelli or twists (about 2-1/2 cups uncooked)
1 lb. fresh asparagus
1 carrot, peeled, julienned
2 to 3 oz. prosciutto, coarsely chopped
1/2 cup plain low-fat yogurt
1 teaspoon finely chopped fresh sage
1/4 teaspoon salt
1/8 teaspoon pepper
1/2 cup shredded mozzarella cheese
1/3 cup bottled honey-Dijon salad dressing

Cook pasta according to package directions; drain. Rinse
with cold water; drain and cool. Trim asparagus, discarding
tough ends. Cut into 1-inch pieces. Cook asparagus and
julienned carrot in boiling water until barely tender; drain
and cool. In a large salad bowl, combine asparagus, carrot,
prosciutto, yogurt, sage, salt and pepper. Add cooled cooked
pasta and mozzarella. Pour salad dressing over all. Toss until
well-blended. Makes 4 to 6 servings.

Pepperoni & Cheese Toss

Count on four main-dish servings or six side salads.

**8 oz. medium shells or macaroni (2-1/4 to 2-1/2
    cups uncooked)**
1 (6-oz.) jar marinated artichoke hearts, quartered, drained
4 to 5 oz. pepperoni, cut into 1/2-inch cubes
1 small red onion, sliced
1/2 cup sliced ripe olives
1 cup shredded mozzarella cheese (4 oz.)
1/2 cup thinly sliced fennel
1/4 cup olive oil or vegetable oil
2 tablespoons red-wine vinegar
1/4 teaspoon salt
1/8 teaspoon pepper

Cook pasta according to package directions; drain. Rinse
with cold water; drain and cool. In a large serving bowl,
combine cooled cooked pasta, artichoke hearts, pepperoni,
onion, olives, mozzarella cheese and fennel. Add oil,
vinegar, salt and pepper. Toss until well-blended.
Makes 4 to 6 servings.

Skillet Combos

The skillet combinations of pasta with other foods result in a quick-and-easy variety of favorite dishes. While the ziti, penne, or elbow-shaped pasta cooks in a large pan of boiling water, quickly sauté some sausage or strips of pork with several of your favorite vegetables and fresh herbs. Stir in a few ingredients and the sauce will be done when the pasta is cooked!

Creamy Gorgonzola Pasta

We enjoy Gorgonzola cheese in this dish; Roquefort, blue or Stilton cheese could be substituted.

8 oz. angel hair or spaghettini
2 tablespoons margarine or butter
1 garlic clove, crushed
4 green onions, cut into 1/4-inch slices
1 cup sliced mushrooms
1-1/2 cups crumbled Gorgonzola cheese (about 6 oz.)
1/8 teaspoon pepper
1/2 cup dairy sour cream
2 tablespoons coarsely chopped watercress

Cook pasta according to package directions; drain. While pasta cooks, heat margarine or butter in a 10-inch skillet. Add garlic, green onions and mushrooms. Cook and stir until mushrooms are soft. Remove from heat; stir in Gorgonzola, drained cooked pasta, pepper, sour cream and watercress. Makes 4 or 5 servings.

Skillet Ziti with Smoked Sausage

Flavorful smoked sausage provides the basic seasoning for this popular dish.

8 oz. ziti or large elbow macaroni (about 3 cups uncooked)
8 oz. smoked sausage, diced
1 onion, chopped
2 tablespoons all-purpose flour
2 cups milk
6 oz. shredded Monterey Jack cheese (1-1/2 cups
    loosely packed)
1 garlic clove, crushed
1/2 cup sliced mushrooms
1/4 teaspoon salt
1/8 teaspoon pepper

Cook pasta according to package directions; drain. Rinse with hot water; drain and set aside. In a large skillet, heat smoked sausage and onion. Add flour; stir and cook 2 minutes. Stir in milk; stir over medium heat until thickened and bubbly. Add cheese, drained cooked pasta, garlic, mushrooms, salt and pepper. Heat until bubbly. Makes 4 to 6 servings.

Sweet-Hot Chicken Pasta

Save preparation time: buy packages of boneless, skinless chicken breasts already cut into strips.

1/2 cup plum jam
1 tablespoon sweet-hot mustard
2 tablespoons soy sauce
2 tablespoons lemon juice
1/4 to 1/2 teaspoon crushed red-pepper flakes
1 garlic clove, crushed
8 oz. small pasta rings or orzo (1-1/4 to 1-3/4 cups uncooked)
2 tablespoons vegetable oil
4 boneless skinless chicken breasts, cut into thin strips
    (about 1-1/4 lbs.)
1/2 lb. broccoli or broccoflower, coarsely chopped
2 carrots, peeled, shredded
1 (8-oz.) can sliced water chestnuts, drained
1/2 teaspoon salt

In a small bowl, combine plum jam, mustard, soy sauce, lemon juice, red-pepper flakes and garlic; set aside. Cook pasta according to package directions; drain. Rinse with hot water; drain and set aside in a large warm serving bowl. While pasta cooks, heat oil in a large skillet or wok. Add chicken; cook and stir 2 or 3 minutes. Add broccoli, carrots, water chestnuts and salt. Cook 5 to 7 minutes longer or until vegetables are crisp-tender. Add plum-jam mixture and cook until well-mixed and hot. Stir in plum-jam mixture until heated. Spoon chicken mixture over drained cooked pasta. Makes 4 to 6 servings.

Sausage-Mushroom Surprise

Ziti provides a hearty base for this flavorful dish.

8 oz. ziti or mostaccioli (about 3 cups uncooked)
8 oz. regular or spicy bulk pork sausage
1 small onion, chopped
1 tablespoon chopped parsley
1 cup sliced mushrooms
1/4 cup chopped sun-dried tomatoes in oil, drained
1 cup plain low-fat yogurt
1/4 cup grated Parmesan cheese, if desired

Cook pasta according to package directions; drain. Rinse with hot water; drain and set aside. Sauté sausage and onion in a large skillet, breaking meat into small pieces with the back of a fork. Cook until sausage is almost done; drain fat. Add parsley and mushrooms. Cook 2 or 3 minutes. Stir in drained cooked pasta, dried tomatoes and yogurt. Heat but do not boil. Sprinkle with Parmesan cheese, if desired. Makes 4 or 5 servings.

Onion-Fennel Toss

Reserve some uncooked fennel leaves to chop and sprinkle over the top of the finished pasta dish.

8 oz. medium shells or twists (about 2-1/2 cups uncooked)
2 tablespoons vegetable oil
1 fennel bulb, thinly sliced (about 12 oz.)
1 onion, thinly sliced
1 cup chicken broth or bouillon
1 (12-oz.) can evaporated skimmed milk
1/4 teaspoon salt
1/8 teaspoon pepper
1 tablespoon cornstarch
2 tablespoons cold water
1 cup shredded Monterey Jack cheese (4 oz.)

Cook pasta according to package directions; drain. Rinse with hot water; drain and set aside. While pasta cooks, heat oil in a large skillet. Add fennel and onion; stir and cook 2 or 3 minutes. Stir in broth or bouillon, evaporated milk, salt and pepper. Simmer 6 to 8 minutes or until vegetables are almost done. Dissolve cornstarch in cold water. Add to vegetable mixture; stir and simmer 2 or 3 minutes. Toss with drained cooked pasta and cheese. Makes 4 or 5 servings.

Skillet Orzo

Use a skillet with a tight-fitting lid to hold in the steam that cooks pasta and vegetables.

1 small onion, chopped
1 small green or red bell pepper, chopped
1 tablespoon vegetable oil
1 garlic clove, crushed
1 jalapeño pepper, chopped
1 (11-1/2-oz.) can vegetable-juice cocktail
1 teaspoon chili powder
1 teaspoon beef-bouillon granules or 1 cube
1/2 teaspoon salt
1 cup orzo or small stars
1/2 cup shredded Monterey Jack or Cheddar cheese
1 tablespoon chopped cilantro

In a 10-inch skillet, combine onion, bell pepper and oil. Cook over medium heat, stirring occasionally, 2 to 3 minutes. Add garlic, jalapeño pepper, vegetable juice, chili powder, beef bouillon granules or crumbled cube, salt and uncooked pasta. Cover and cook over low heat 10 to 12 minutes or until pasta is tender. Sprinkle with cheese and cilantro. Makes 5 or 6 servings.

Prosciutto Linguine Toss

The wonderful flavor of prosciutto blends with other ingredients to create one of our favorite dishes.

8 oz. linguine or fettucine
2 tablespoons margarine or butter
3 to 4 oz. prosciutto, cut into bite-size pieces
1 cup sliced mushrooms
1 cup cooked peas
1 cup dairy sour cream
1/4 cup grated Parmesan or Romano cheese
1/4 teaspoon salt
1/8 teaspoon pepper
Chopped Italian parsley
Additional grated Parmesan or Romano cheese, if desired

Cook pasta according to package directions; drain. Rinse with hot water; drain and set aside in a large warm serving bowl. While pasta cooks, melt margarine or butter in a large skillet; add prosciutto, mushrooms and peas. Stir in sour cream, cheese, salt and pepper; heat until bubbly. Spoon over drained cooked pasta; toss until well-mixed. Sprinkle with chopped Italian parsley and additional cheese, if desired. Makes 4 to 6 servings.

Italian-Sausage Pasta Toss

A hearty dish with a compatible combination of flavors.

8 oz. penne or spiral pasta (about 2-1/2 cups uncooked)
8 oz. Italian sausage
1 leek, chopped
1 cup coarsely chopped mushrooms
1 cup chicken broth or bouillon
1 cup fresh or frozen peas
1/4 cup grated Romano or Parmesan cheese
2 tablespoons seasoned dry bread crumbs

Cook pasta according to package directions; drain. Rinse with hot water; drain and set aside. While pasta cooks, remove and discard sausage casing. Break sausage into small pieces. Cook in a 10-inch skillet with leek; drain fat. Stir in mushrooms, broth or bouillon and peas. Cover and simmer 3 to 4 minutes. Toss with drained cooked pasta. Sprinkle with cheese, then bread crumbs.
Makes 4 or 5 servings.

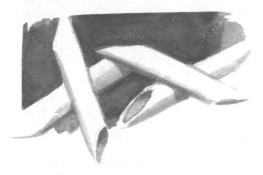

Scallop & Leek Medley

If scallops are large, cut them in half or in thirds for more manageable servings.

8 oz. vermicelli or angel-hair
2 tablespoons vegetable oil
2 leeks, thinly sliced crosswise
1 (10-1/2-oz.) can double-strength chicken broth
1/8 teaspoon red-pepper flakes
1/4 teaspoon salt
1 garlic clove, crushed
8 oz. scallops
2 tablespoons dry white wine
1/2 cup half and half

Cook pasta according to package directions; drain. Rinse with hot water; drain and set aside. While pasta cooks, heat oil in a large skillet. Add leeks; cook and stir over medium-high heat 2 or 3 minutes. Stir in chicken broth, red-pepper flakes, salt, garlic and scallops. Simmer 4 or 5 minutes. Stir in wine, half and half and drained cooked pasta.
Makes 4 or 5 servings.

Mandarin Stir-Fry Pork Dinner

Cook all the colorful basic ingredients in your wok or favorite large skillet.

8 oz. bucatini or linguine
2 tablespoons vegetable oil
8 oz. lean uncooked boneless pork, cut into bite-size pieces
1 red onion, sliced
2 carrots, peeled, thinly sliced
1/4 teaspoon salt
1/8 teaspoon pepper
1 cup fresh pea pods (about 2-1/2 oz.)
1 cup chicken broth
2 tablespoons cornstarch
2 tablespoons soy sauce
1 cup orange juice
1 (11-oz.) can mandarin oranges, drained
1/4 cup toasted slivered almonds

Cook pasta according to package directions; drain. Rinse with hot water; drain and set aside. While pasta cooks, heat oil in a large skillet or wok. Add pork, onion, carrots, salt and pepper. Stir and cook several minutes or until tender. Stir in pea pods. In a small bowl, combine chicken broth, cornstarch, soy sauce and orange juice. Add to pan; cook and stir until thickened slightly. Add mandarin oranges. Stir drained cooked pasta into cooked meat-and-vegetable mixture. Top with almonds. Makes 4 or 5 servings.

Skillet Chicken & Pasta with Avocado Sauce

For variety, substitute fresh nectarines or peaches for oranges.

1 large ripe avocado, peeled, cubed
1/3 cup dairy sour cream
1 teaspoon lemon juice
1 teaspoon honey
1/8 teaspoon paprika
1 tablespoon chopped fresh or canned green chili pepper
8 oz. medium noodles
4 boneless skinless chicken-breast halves
2 tablespoons vegetable oil
2 green onions, sliced
1/4 teaspoon salt
1 teaspoon sesame seeds
Sliced oranges

In a blender or food processor, combine avocado, sour cream, lemon juice, honey, paprika and chili pepper; process until well-blended. Set aside. Cook pasta according to package directions; drain. Rinse with hot water; drain and set aside. While pasta cooks, cut chicken into 2" x 1/2" strips. Heat oil in a large skillet. Add chicken, green onions, salt and sesame seeds. Cook and stir 2 or 3 minutes or until chicken is firm and white. On a large platter, spoon cooked chicken over drained cooked pasta. Top with avocado sauce. Garnish with sliced oranges. Makes 4 or 5 servings.

Eggplant Macaroni Skillet

A compatible combination of Italian flavors enhances this skillet recipe.

8 oz. large elbow macaroni or ziti (2-1/2 to
    3 cups uncooked)
2 tablespoons vegetable oil
1 eggplant, unpeeled, cut into 1/2-inch cubes
1 small onion, diced
1 garlic clove, crushed
1/4 teaspoon salt
2 to 3 oz. prosciutto, chopped (about 1/2 cup)
1/4 teaspoon red-pepper flakes
1 (8-oz.) can tomato sauce
1/4 teaspoon ground nutmeg
1/2 cup half and half or light cream
1/4 cup grated Romano or Parmesan cheese

Cook pasta according to package directions; drain. Rinse with hot water; drain and set aside. While pasta cooks, heat oil in a large skillet. Add eggplant, onion, garlic, salt, prosciutto, red-pepper flakes, tomato sauce and nutmeg. Cover and simmer 15 to 20 minutes or until eggplant is tender. Stir in half and half or cream and heat to desired temperature. Stir drained cooked pasta into eggplant mixture. Sprinkle with Romano or Parmesan cheese. Makes 4 to 6 servings.

Leek Twists

Use the white and light-green part of leeks. Discard the tough dark-green leaves.

8 oz. twists or spiral pasta (about 2-1/4 cups uncooked)
1 tablespoon vegetable oil
2 leeks, thinly sliced
1/4 teaspoon salt
1/8 teaspoon pepper
1/4 cup loosely packed watercress leaves
1 cup ricotta cheese (8 oz.)
1/4 teaspoon grated lemon peel
1/4 cup crumbled blue or Gorgonzola cheese

Cook pasta according to package directions; drain. Rinse with hot water; drain and set aside. While pasta cooks, heat oil in a large skillet. Add leeks, salt and pepper. Cook and stir over low heat 6 to 8 minutes or until leeks are limp. Stir in watercress. Remove from heat and stir in ricotta, lemon peel and drained cooked pasta. Sprinkle crumbled cheese over all. Makes 4 to 5 servings.

Chicken & Orzo with Gingered Apricot-Almond Topping

Orzo pasta is shaped like rice; it combines well with poultry.

1 tablespoon vegetable oil
1 lb. boneless skinless chicken breasts or thighs,
    cut into bite-size pieces
1 leek, finely chopped
1/4 cup chopped red bell pepper
5 oz. orzo or small pasta rings (3/4 cup uncooked)
2 cups chicken broth or bouillon
1/2 teaspoon grated fresh ginger
1/2 cup canned apricot halves, drained, chopped
1/4 cup toasted slivered almonds, chopped

In a large skillet, heat oil. Add chicken, leek and bell pepper. Stir and cook 2 or 3 minutes. Add uncooked pasta and chicken broth or bouillon. Cover and simmer 20 minutes. Combine ginger and apricots. Spoon over cooked pasta. Top with toasted almonds.
Makes 4 or 5 servings.

Light & Healthy Choices

Pasta is naturally low in fat, yet high in complex carbohydrates. For healthy eating, choose sauces or companion ingredients that are light and nutritious.

In many recipes, you can stretch calories and reduce fat by using less meat or cheese than the original recipe requires, then increasing the fresh vegetables.

Rich creamy sauces have a reputation of being high in calories and fat. We discovered that evaporated skimmed milk reduces total calories and fat, yet provides a smooth rich texture when substituted for whipping cream in a sauce.

Quick Ravioli Soup

A package of refrigerated pasta is handy to have on hand to combine with vegetables for a quick and healthy meal.

7 cups beef broth or bouillon
1 small sweet potato, peeled, halved, thinly sliced
1 tablespoon soy sauce
1 garlic clove, crushed
1 (9-oz.) pkg. refrigerated cheese ravioli
3 cups Savoy cabbage cut into thin strips

In a large pan or Dutch oven, combine broth or bouillon, sweet potato, soy sauce and garlic. Bring to boil; add refrigerated ravioli. Simmer 4 minutes. Stir in Savoy cabbage; simmer 2 minutes longer or until cabbage is tender. Makes 5 or 6 servings.

Fresh Herbed Tomato Pasta

A combination of the best fresh herbs with garden-grown tomatoes for a quick pasta dish.

8 oz. small shells or salad macaroni (about 2-1/2 cups uncooked)
4 tomatoes, chopped
2 tablespoons finely chopped fresh basil
2 green onions, finely chopped
2 tablespoons finely chopped Italian parsley
1 teaspoon finely chopped fresh oregano
1 garlic clove, crushed
1/4 teaspoon salt
1/8 teaspoon pepper
1/4 cup olive oil
1 tablespoon red-wine vinegar

Cook pasta according to package directions; drain. Rinse with hot water; drain and set aside. While pasta cooks, combine tomatoes, basil, green onions, parsley, oregano, garlic, salt, pepper, oil and vinegar in a large serving bowl. Add drained cooked pasta; toss until well-blended. Makes 4 to 6 servings.

Roasted-Pepper Seafood Toss

For a pleasant flavor change, substitute halved or quartered cooked scallops for the shrimp.

8 oz. fusilli or spaghetti
4 yellow, orange or red bell peppers
2 tablespoons vegetable oil
2 green onions, coarsely chopped
1/2 teaspoon salt
1/4 teaspoon pepper
1 (12-oz.) can evaporated skimmed milk
1/4 cup cilantro leaves
8 oz. cooked shelled medium shrimp

Cook pasta according to package directions; drain. Rinse with hot water; drain and set aside in a large serving bowl. While pasta cooks, preheat oven to 475F (245C). Place whole peppers on a shallow baking sheet. Roast in preheated oven 20 to 25 minutes or until browned and blistered. Cool; remove and discard stems, seeds and skins. Combine pepper flesh in a food processor or blender with oil, green onions, salt, pepper, evaporated milk and cilantro. Process until finely chopped. Stir in cooked shelled shrimp. Spoon over drained cooked pasta; toss until well-blended.
Makes 4 to 6 servings.

Pesto Pasta with Chicken

It's equally delicious served hot or at room temperature.

8 oz. fettucine or linguine
2 boneless skinless chicken-breast halves, cooked
2 medium tomatoes, coarsely chopped
1/4 cup chopped fresh basil
1 garlic clove, crushed
1/4 cup olive oil
1/4 teaspoon salt
1/8 teaspoon pepper
1/2 cup toasted pine nuts

Cook pasta according to package directions; drain. Rinse with warm water; drain and set aside. While pasta cooks, cut cooked chicken into strips about 1/2" x 1". In a small bowl, combine tomatoes, basil, garlic, oil, salt and pepper. Chop half the pine nuts and add to tomato mixture. Reserve remaining pine nuts. In a large serving bowl, combine cooked chicken, tomato mixture and drained cooked pasta; toss until well-blended. Top with remaining toasted pine nuts. Makes 4 to 6 servings.

Festive Confetti Salad

For a heartier main dish, top salad with small cooked shrimp or sliced cooked scallops.

8 oz. fusilli or linguine
1 yellow bell pepper, thinly sliced
1 red bell pepper, thinly sliced
1 (8-oz.) can water chestnuts, drained, sliced
4 green onions, sliced
1 cup Chinese pea pods
2 cups bean sprouts
1/4 cup white-wine vinegar
3 tablespoons vegetable oil
1 tablespoon sesame oil
2 tablespoons soy sauce
1 garlic clove, crushed
1 small bunch enoki mushrooms

Cook pasta according to package directions; drain. Rinse with cold water; drain. In a large serving bowl, combine drained cooked pasta, bell peppers, water chestnuts, green onions, pea pods and bean sprouts. In a small bowl, combine vinegar, vegetable oil, sesame oil, soy sauce and garlic. Pour over pasta mixture; toss until well-blended. Top with enoki mushrooms. Makes 6 or 7 servings.

Shrimp & Shells Cocktail

A wonderful-tasting way to stretch shrimp.

6 oz. small shells (about 1-2/3 cup uncooked)
2 tablespoons vegetable oil
1/4 cup white-wine vinegar
1 teaspoon Worcestershire sauce
1 tablespoon chopped cilantro
1 garlic clove, crushed
1/4 teaspoon seasoned salt
1 small (mild) California green chili, seeded, chopped
1/3 lb. small cooked shelled shrimp
4 to 6 lettuce leaves
2 hard-cooked eggs, chopped

Cook pasta according to package directions; drain. Rinse with cold water; drain and cool. In a large serving bowl, combine oil, vinegar, Worcestershire sauce, cilantro, garlic, seasoned salt and chili pepper. Stir in cooked shrimp and pasta. Cover and refrigerate at least 1 hour. Serve in lettuce-lined cocktail glasses or salad plates. Sprinkle with hard-cooked eggs. Makes 4 to 6 servings.

Garden-Vegetable Special

The colorful combination of fresh vegetables means healthy dining with an eye-appealing main dish.

8 oz. cavatelli or spiral pasta (about 2-1/2 cups uncooked)
2 tablespoons olive oil
2 carrots, peeled, thinly sliced diagonally
1 red onion, sliced into rings
1/2 small head cauliflower, cut into small flowerets
(about 2 cups)
2 zucchini, cut into 2-inch sticks
1 red or yellow bell pepper, cut into 1-inch cubes
2 fresh tomatoes, peeled, seeded, diced
2 tablespoons chopped fresh basil
2 tablespoons chopped cilantro
1/4 teaspoon salt
1/8 teaspoon crushed red-pepper flakes
2 tablespoons grated Parmesan cheese

Cook pasta according to package directions; drain. Rinse with hot water; drain and set aside. While pasta cooks, heat oil in a large skillet. Add carrots and onion. Cook and stir 3 or 4 minutes. Stir in cauliflower, zucchini, bell pepper, tomatoes, basil, cilantro, salt and red-pepper flakes. Cover and simmer 8 to 10 minutes or until vegetables are crisp-tender. Stir in drained cooked pasta. Sprinkle with Parmesan cheese. Makes 5 or 6 servings.

Green & Gold Spaghettini

Looks great—tastes wonderful—and it's good for you!

8 oz. spaghettini or capellini
1 tablespoon vegetable oil or olive oil
8 oz. lean ground chicken or turkey
3 yellow crookneck or pattypan squash, sliced
1 leek, thinly sliced
1 tomato, chopped
1/2 teaspoon salt
1/8 teaspoon pepper
2 tablespoons watercress, coarsely chopped
1/2 cup plain low-fat yogurt
1 tablespoon Dijon-style mustard
2 tablespoons grated Parmesan cheese, if desired

Cook pasta according to package directions; drain. Rinse with hot water; drain and set aside. While pasta cooks, heat oil in a large skillet. Add ground chicken or turkey. Heat and stir until crumbled and almost done; add squash and leek. Cook 3 to 5 minutes; stir in tomato, salt, pepper, watercress, yogurt and mustard. Add drained cooked pasta. Sprinkle with cheese, if desired. Makes 6 or 7 servings.

Peppered Squash with Tortelloni

Use refrigerated tortelloni and fresh vegetables for a hearty main dish.

1 (9-oz.) pkg. chicken tortelloni
1 tablespoon vegetable oil
1 garlic clove, crushed
2 large zucchini, sliced
1 red bell pepper, julienned
2 green onions, sliced
1 (8-oz.) can tomato sauce
1/2 teaspoon salt
1/8 teaspoon pepper
1 tablespoon chopped fresh basil
1 tablespoon white-wine Worcestershire sauce
1 tablespoon finely chopped parsley
2 tablespoons grated Parmesan or Romano cheese

Cook pasta according to package directions; drain. Rinse with hot water; drain and set aside. Heat oil in a large skillet. Add garlic, zucchini, bell pepper, green onions, tomato sauce, salt and pepper. Cook and stir until vegetables are crisp-tender. Add basil, Worcestershire sauce, parsley and drained cooked pasta. Sprinkle with cheese. Makes 4 or 5 servings.

Microwave Timesavers

Microwaving is in step with today's hectic lifestyle. It saves time without compromising the good taste of food. However, before I rave about the wonders of microwaving, let me make it very clear that I do not believe that cooking pasta is one of its virtues. Uncooked pasta can be cooked just as quickly by the traditional boiling-water-in-a-large-pan method.

On the other hand, the microwave is a whiz at saving time and energy in making sauces and toppings, thawing frozen casseroles and heating pasta dishes that are made early in the day to be served at the evening meal.

To make the most of your time, microwave the sauce while pasta cooks. Then combine the sauce and cooked pasta as we did in Spoonburger Pasta or Busy-Day Chili-Mac.

Macaroni & Cheese with Cherry Tomatoes

An unbelievably quick and easy dish.

8 oz. elbow macaroni or ziti (about 3 cups uncooked)
1 (16-oz.) jar pasteurized process-cheese spread
1 cup cherry tomatoes, halved or quartered
1/3 cup crumbled cooked bacon or boiled ham

Cook pasta according to package directions; drain. Rinse with hot water; drain and set aside in a large warm serving bowl. While pasta cooks, remove lid from cheese spread. Microwave in open jar on HIGH 2 to 2-1/2 minutes, stirring 2 or 3 times. Mix drained cooked pasta, hot cheese spread and tomatoes. Top with bacon or ham. Makes 4 or 5 servings.

Spoonburger Pasta

Quick and easy microwaveable ingredients that you can add to your favorite cooked pasta.

8 oz. medium noodles or bow ties (4 to 4-1/2 cups uncooked)
1 lb. lean ground beef
1 small onion, chopped
2 (8-oz.) cans tomato sauce
2 teaspoons brown sugar
1 teaspoon chili powder
2 teaspoons Worcestershire sauce
1/4 teaspoon salt
1/2 cup shredded Cheddar cheese

Cook pasta according to package directions; drain. Rinse with hot water; drain and set aside in a large warm serving bowl. While pasta cooks, microwave beef and onion in a 2-1/2-quart microwaveable dish on HIGH 8 to 10 minutes. Stir several times to break up meat. Drain excess fat. Add tomato sauce, brown sugar, chili powder, Worcestershire sauce and salt to dish. Heat in microwave on HIGH 1-1/2 to 2 minutes. Spoon over drained cooked noodles. Sprinkle with cheese. Makes 4 to 6 servings.

Curried Shrimp & Shells

A tried-and-true favorite combination of shrimp and curry provides the base for this quick main dish.

8 oz. medium shells or elbow macaroni (about 3 cups uncooked)
1 tablespoon cornstarch
1 (12-oz.) can evaporated skimmed milk or half and half
1-1/2 teaspoons curry powder
1/4 teaspoon ground ginger
1 teaspoon lemon juice
1/4 teaspoon salt
8 oz. cooked shelled medium shrimp
2 teaspoons chopped chives

Cook pasta according to package directions; drain. Rinse with hot water; drain. While pasta cooks, combine cornstarch, evaporated milk or half and half, curry powder, ginger, lemon juice and salt in a microwaveable bowl. Microwave on HIGH about 3 minutes or until bubbly, stirring at least once. Add cooked shrimp and drained cooked pasta; toss until well-blended. Sprinkle with chives. Makes 4 or 5 servings.

Hot German Pasta Salad with Kielbasa

A very satisfying main-dish pasta salad with popular sweet-sour flavors.

8 oz. ziti or rigatoni (3 to 3-1/2 cups uncooked)
3 bacon slices, chopped
1 medium onion, chopped
2 tablespoons all-purpose flour
1 tablespoon sugar
1 teaspoon dry mustard
1/4 teaspoon celery seeds
1/2 teaspoon salt
1/8 teaspoon pepper
1/4 cup white-wine vinegar
3/4 cup water
1 lb. smoked Polish sausage (kielbasa) cut into 8 to 10 pieces

Cook pasta according to package directions; drain. Rinse with hot water; drain. While pasta cooks, microwave bacon and onion in a microwaveable 1-quart cup or bowl on HIGH 4 or 5 minutes or until done. Stir in flour, sugar, mustard, celery seeds, salt and pepper, then vinegar and water. Microwave on HIGH 2 or 3 minutes longer, stirring once; set aside. Place sausage in a 2-quart microwaveable dish. Cover with waxed paper. Microwave on HIGH 3 minutes. Stir in drained cooked pasta and sauce. Makes 4 to 6 servings.

Busy-Day Chili-Mac

Keep the pasta and canned vegetables on hand for an impromptu hearty lunch or dinner.

8 oz. medium shells or elbow macaroni (2 to 2-1/2 cups uncooked)
2 (15-oz.) cans chili without beans
1 (4-oz.) can diced green chili peppers, drained
1 (14-to 16-oz.) can diced peeled tomatoes
1 to 1-1/2 cups shredded Monterey Jack cheese (4 to 6 oz.)
2 green onions, chopped

Cook pasta according to package directions; drain. Rinse with hot water; drain and set aside. In a 2-1/2-quart microwaveable bowl, microwave chili, green chili peppers and tomatoes on HIGH 6-1/2 to 7 minutes, stirring twice. Stir in drained cooked pasta. Serve in individual soup bowls. Sprinkle with cheese and green onions.
Makes 4 or 5 servings.

Microwaved Stroganoff Noodles

Cook the noodles the traditional way. Save time by microwaving the sauce.

8 oz. wide noodles
2 tablespoons vegetable oil
1 lb. boneless beef sirloin, cut into 1/2" x 2" pieces
1/3 cup all-purpose flour
1 onion, chopped
1 cup sliced mushrooms
1 (14-1/2-oz.) can beef broth
2 teaspoons Worcestershire sauce
2 tablespoons tomato paste
1/2 teaspoon salt
1/4 teaspoon pepper
1 cup dairy sour cream

Cook pasta according to package directions; drain. Rinse with hot water; drain and set aside. While pasta cooks, heat oil in a 3-quart microwaveable casserole on HIGH 1 minute. Coat beef with flour; add to hot oil in casserole. Microwave on HIGH 2 minutes. Turn beef and add onion. Microwave on HIGH 2 minutes. Stir in mushrooms, beef broth, Worcestershire sauce, tomato paste, salt and pepper. Cover and microwave on HIGH 4 minutes. In a small bowl, stir about 1/2 cup hot mixture into sour cream, then add to casserole. Stir in drained cooked noodles.
Makes 5 or 6 servings.

Hurry-Up Cheese-Dog Soup

Microwave a 10-ounce package of frozen chopped broccoli; let it drain in a strainer or colander while the pasta cooks.

8 oz. cavatelli or cavatappi (about 2-1/2 cups uncooked)
8 oz. pasteurized process cheese spread, cubed
3 cups low-fat milk
1 teaspoon prepared mustard
1 to 1-1/2 cups drained cooked, chopped broccoli
4 hot dogs, thinly sliced
1 green onion, thinly sliced

Cook pasta according to package directions; drain. Rinse with hot water; drain and set aside. While pasta cooks, combine cheese spread, milk and mustard in a 2-1/2-quart microwaveable bowl. Microwave on HIGH about 4-1/2 minutes or until cheese melts. Add cooked broccoli and hot dogs. Microwave on HIGH 1-1/2 to 2 minutes or until bubbly. Stir in drained cooked pasta. Sprinkle with green onion. Makes 5 or 6 servings.

Speedy Spicy Toss

Choose salsa with the right amount of "heat" for your family.

8 oz. spaghetti or noodles
1 (28-oz.) can crushed tomatoes with added puree
2 teaspoons chicken-bouillon granules
1/2 teaspoon chili powder
1 (8-oz.) jar chunky salsa (1 cup)
1/2 teaspoon salt
1 tablespoon chopped cilantro
1/2 cup shredded Monterey Jack cheese, if desired

Cook pasta according to package directions; drain. Rinse
with hot water; drain and set aside in a large warm serving
bowl. While pasta cooks, combine tomatoes, chicken-
bouillon granules, chili powder, salsa, salt and cilantro in a
2-1/2-quart microwaveable bowl. Microwave on HIGH
3 to 3-1/2 minutes or until bubbly. Pour over drained cooked
pasta; toss until well-mixed. Sprinkle with cheese, if desired.
Makes about 6 cups.

Timesaver's Marinara Sausage Dish

Containers of refrigerated marinara sauce are in the deli section of supermarkets or pasta take-out stores.

8 oz. penne or fusilli (about 2-1/2 cups uncooked)
8 oz. Italian sausage or bulk pork sausage
1 garlic clove, crushed
1/4 teaspoon salt
1 (4-oz.) can chopped green chilies, drained
1 (15-oz.) carton refrigerated marinara sauce
1 cup shredded Monterey Jack cheese (4 oz.)

Cook pasta according to package directions; drain. Rinse with hot water; drain and set aside in a large warm serving bowl. While pasta cooks, break up sausage in a 2-1/2-quart microwaveable dish. Microwave on HIGH 2-1/2 to 3 minutes, stirring once. Drain most of the fat. Add garlic, salt, green chilies and marinara sauce. Microwave on HIGH 2 minutes or until bubbly. Toss with drained cooked pasta. Sprinkle with cheese. Makes 4 or 5 servings.

Smoky-Cheese Corkscrews with Asparagus

A timesaving main dish with an enticing smoky flavor.

8 oz. corkscrews or cavatelli (about 2-1/2 cups uncooked)
2 shallots, finely chopped
1 tablespoon margarine or butter
4 oz. shredded, hickory-smoked, pasteurized, process
**   Cheddar cheese (about 1/2 cup)**
1 (12-oz.) can evaporated skimmed milk
1 (10-oz.) pkg. frozen cut asparagus, cooked, drained
1/4 teaspoon salt
1/8 teaspoon pepper

Cook pasta according to package directions; drain. Rinse with hot water; drain and set aside. While pasta cooks, combine shallots and margarine or butter in a 2-1/2-quart microwaveable dish. Microwave on HIGH 3 minutes or until shallots are softened. Stir in cheese, milk, cooked asparagus, salt and pepper. Microwave on MEDIUM 4-1/2 to 5 minutes or until hot. Stir in drained cooked pasta.
Makes 4 to 6 servings.

Ethnic Flavors

Many people think of pasta as an Italian food. That might have been true many years ago. Today, pasta is used as a partner with foods around the world. It blends flavors borrowed from a wide variety of cultures. A little ingenuity results in exciting combinations.

There's the Bangkok Chicken & Noodles featuring a sauce spiced with jalapeño pepper and cilantro, with a hint of peanut and soy flavors. From south-of-the-border is Layered Chili Rellenos Macaroni, a baked pasta dish. European food favorites are featured in the Greek Island Toss and Rhineland Pasta. All of these recipes are great for ethnic dinner parties.

Salsa Chicken Bake with Orzo

Use your family's favorite salsa.

1 cup orzo
1 (24-oz.) jar chunky salsa
1 cup ricotta cheese (8 oz.)
6 chicken thighs
1 cup shredded Monterey Jack cheese (4 oz.)
1/2 cup soft bread crumbs
2 tablespoons melted margarine or butter
1 avocado, peeled, sliced

Preheat oven to 375F (190C). Combine uncooked orzo, salsa and ricotta in the bottom of an 11" x 8" baking dish. Top with chicken thighs, then cheese. Combine bread crumbs and margarine or butter; sprinkle over all. Bake in preheated oven 40 to 45 minutes. Garnish with avocado slices. Makes 6 servings.

Rhineland Pasta

Old-World flavors in a hearty stick-to-the-ribs main dish.

8 oz. ziti or mostaccioli (about 3 cups uncooked)
8 oz. knockwurst, cut into 1/4-inch-thick diagonal slices
1 large onion, thinly sliced
3 tablespoons vegetable oil
1/4 cup all-purpose flour
2 cups milk
1 tablespoon German-style or spicy brown mustard
1 teaspoon horseradish
1/4 teaspoon salt
1/8 teaspoon pepper
1 cup shredded Muenster or Swiss cheese (4 oz.)

Cook pasta according to package directions; drain. Rinse
with hot water; drain and set aside. In a large skillet, sauté
sliced knockwurst and onion in oil until onion is limp. Stir in
flour; cook 2 minutes. Add milk, mustard, horseradish, salt
and pepper. Cook and stir over low heat until thickened. Add
drained cooked pasta. Top with cheese. Heat until melted or
place under broiler until golden brown and bubbly.
Makes 4 to 6 servings.

Bangkok Chicken & Noodles

Peanut butter is a flavor surprise.

8 oz. fine noodles or capellini
2 tablespoons vegetable oil
1 garlic clove, crushed
4 or 5 boneless skinless chicken-breast halves
1/4 cup crunchy peanut butter
2 tablespoons soy sauce
1 tablespoon brown sugar
1/4 cup orange juice
1 jalapeño pepper, seeded, finely chopped
1 cup chicken broth or bouillon
1 tablespoon cornstarch
2 tablespoons white wine
1 tablespoon chopped cilantro

Cook pasta according to package directions; drain. Rinse with hot water; drain and set aside. While pasta cooks, heat oil and garlic in a large skillet. Add chicken and sauté on both sides. In a small bowl, thoroughly combine peanut butter, soy sauce and brown sugar. Stir in orange juice, jalapeño pepper, broth or bouillon, cornstarch and wine. Pour over chicken; cover and simmer over low heat 6 to 8 minutes or until tender. Spoon drained cooked pasta onto a serving plate. Top with chicken and sauce. Sprinkle with cilantro. Makes 4 or 5 servings.

Layered Chili Rellenos Macaroni

A pleasant chili flavor, not too spicy.

8 oz. small elbow or shell macaroni (2 to 2-1/4 cups uncooked)
1 (4-oz.) can chopped green chilies, drained
6 oz. shredded Cheddar cheese (about 2 cups)
2 medium zucchini, julienned
3 eggs, beaten slightly
3/4 cup plain low-fat yogurt
1 teaspoon prepared mustard
1/2 teaspoon salt
1 green onion, finely chopped

Cook pasta according to package directions; drain. Rinse with hot water; drain and set aside. Grease a 2-1/2-quart baking dish. Arrange half of drained cooked pasta on bottom of baking dish. Top with chilies and half of shredded cheese, then zucchini and remaining pasta. In a medium bowl, Combine eggs, yogurt, mustard, salt and green onion; spoon over all. Sprinkle with remaining cheese. Preheat oven to 350F (175C). Bake 35 to 45 minutes or until firm.
Makes 5 or 6 servings.

Pork Stir-Fry with Chinese Noodles

A quick and easy stir-fry featuring crispy chow-mein noodles.

1 tablespoon vegetable oil
8 oz. boneless pork cutlets, cut into 1/2" x 2" strips
1 cup broccoli, cut into thin slices
1 cup yellow crookneck squash, sliced
1 red bell pepper, sliced
1 cup sliced mushrooms
3 green onions, cut into 1/2-inch lengths
1 cup chicken broth
2 tablespoons cornstarch
2 tablespoons soy sauce
1 teaspoon grated fresh ginger
2 cups chow-mein noodles

In a large skillet, heat oil. Add pork; stir-fry 1 or 2 minutes. Stir in broccoli and squash; cook and stir 2 minutes. Add bell pepper, mushrooms and green onions. Cook and stir another minute. In a small bowl, combine chicken broth, cornstarch, soy and ginger. Add to vegetables; cook and stir until bubbly and thickened. Spoon over chow-mein noodles. Makes 4 to 6 servings.

Italian Sampler

Porcini mushrooms' distinctive flavor enhances this Italian-inspired dish.

1 (about 1-oz.) pkg. dried porcini mushrooms
8 oz. rotelle or fettucine
2 tablespoons olive oil
1 garlic clove, crushed
1/4 cup coarsely chopped fresh basil
2 green onions, sliced
1/2 teaspoon salt
1/8 teaspoon pepper
1 (15-oz.) can cut peeled tomatoes
3 oz. prosciutto, cut into strips 2" x 1/2" (about 1/2 cup)
Grated Parmesan or Romano cheese

Soak porcini mushrooms in warm water 30 minutes. Cook pasta according to package directions; drain. Rinse with hot water; drain and set aside in a large warm bowl. While pasta cooks, heat oil and garlic in a large skillet. Stir in basil, green onions, salt and pepper; cook and stir 2 minutes. Line a medium strainer with paper coffee filter. Strain soaked mushrooms in filter. Reserve 1/2 cup strained liquid; coarsely chop soaked mushrooms; add to skillet. Stir in reserved liquid, tomatoes and prosciutto. Simmer uncovered 15 minutes. Pour over drained cooked pasta; toss until well-blended. Sprinkle with cheese. Makes 4 or 5 servings.

Greek-Island Toss

A special dish for everyone who loves flavors borrowed from the Mediterranean islands.

8 oz. fettucine or linguine
1/2 cup crumbled feta cheese (about 3-1/2 oz.)
1 (2-1/4-oz.) can sliced ripe olives, drained
1 garlic clove, crushed
2 green onions, sliced
1/4 cup chopped sun-dried tomatoes
2 tablespoons chopped parsley
3/4 cup plain low-fat yogurt
1/4 teaspoon salt
1/8 teaspoon pepper
2 tablespoons toasted pine nuts

Cook pasta according to package directions; drain. Rinse with hot water; drain and set aside in a large warm serving bowl. In a medium bowl, combine feta cheese, olives, garlic, green onions, sun-dried tomatoes, parsley, yogurt, salt and pepper. Spoon over drained cooked pasta; toss until well-blended. Sprinkle with pine nuts. Makes about 4 servings.

Rising-Sun Stir Fry

Frozen Oriental-style vegetable combinations vary according to the brand; choose your favorite mixture.

8 oz. spaghettini or vermicelli
1 tablespoon vegetable oil
1 garlic clove, crushed
2 whole boneless skinless chicken breasts, julienned
1/4 cup soy sauce
1/2 teaspoon grated fresh ginger
1 teaspoon sesame oil
1 cup chicken broth or bouillon
1 (16-oz.) pkg. frozen Oriental- or California-style vegetables
2 tablespoons cornstarch
2 tablespoons water

Cook pasta according to package directions; drain. Rinse with hot water; drain and set aside. While pasta cooks, heat vegetable oil and garlic in a large skillet. Add chicken; stir-fry 2 minutes. Stir in soy sauce, fresh ginger, sesame oil, chicken broth or bouillon and vegetables. Cover; simmer about 5 minutes or until vegetables are crisp-tender. Dissolve cornstarch in water. Add to vegetable mixture. Cook and stir until thickened. Add drained cooked pasta.
Makes 4 to 6 servings.

Mid-East Favorite

A favorite combination of vegetables with rigatoni results in a hearty main dish.

8 oz. rigatoni or ziti (3 to 3-1/2 cups uncooked)
2 tablespoons olive oil
1 garlic clove, crushed
1 small onion, chopped
1 mild California green chili pepper, seeded, chopped
1 small eggplant, cubed
1 (16-oz.) can diced peeled tomatoes
1 (6-oz.) can tomato paste
1/4 teaspoon ground turmeric
1/2 teaspoon salt
1/8 teaspoon pepper
1/2 teaspoon grated fresh ginger
1/2 cup plain low-fat yogurt, if desired
1 tablespoon chopped cilantro, if desired

Cook pasta according to package directions; drain. Rinse with hot water; drain and set aside. While pasta cooks, heat oil in a large skillet. Add garlic, onion, chili pepper and eggplant; cook over medium heat 2 or 3 minutes. Stir in tomatoes, tomato paste, turmeric, salt, pepper and ginger; cover and simmer 15 to 20 minutes. Stir in drained cooked pasta. Top each serving with yogurt and cilantro, if desired. Makes 6 to 8 servings.

Oriental Flavors Pork Tenderloin

Pork is easier to slice if it is partially frozen.

1/4 cup soy sauce
1/2 teaspoon grated fresh ginger
2 tablespoons orange marmalade
2 tablespoons cornstarch
1 cup orange juice
8 oz. fettucine or medium noodles
3/4 lb. boneless pork tenderloin
2 tablespoons vegetable oil
2 green or yellow bell peppers, thinly sliced
1 cup sugar snap or Chinese pea pods, uncooked
2 carrots, peeled, shredded
2 tablespoons toasted sesame seeds

In a small bowl, combine soy sauce, ginger, marmalade, cornstarch and orange juice; set aside. Cook pasta according to package directions; drain. Rinse with hot water; drain and set aside. While pasta cooks, cut pork into crosswise slices about 1/4 inch thick. Heat oil in a large skillet or wok. Add pork; cook and stir 3 or 4 minutes or until meat loses its pink color. Reduce heat. Add soy sauce mixture, sliced peppers, sugar peas or pea pods and carrots. Stir and cook until sauce thickens. Arrange drained cooked pasta on a large platter. Spoon pork mixture in middle of pasta. Sprinkle with sesame seeds. Makes 5 or 6 servings.

St. Tropez Skillet

Serve with a loaf of crusty French or Italian bread for an easy luncheon or supper.

8 oz. medium pasta shells or radiatore (about 3 cups uncooked)
2 tablespoons vegetable oil
1 medium eggplant, cut into strips about 1/2" x 2"
1 onion coarsely chopped
1 garlic clove, crushed
1 jalapeño pepper, seeded, finely chopped
1/2 teaspoon salt
1/8 teaspoon pepper
1 cup cherry tomatoes, halved
1/4 cup coarsely chopped fresh basil
1/4 cup sliced ripe olives
1/2 cup plain low-fat yogurt

Cook pasta according to package directions; drain. Rinse with hot water; drain and set aside. While pasta cooks, heat oil in a large skillet or wok. Add eggplant, onion, garlic, jalapeño pepper, salt and pepper. Cook and stir until eggplant is soft. Remove from heat. Add tomatoes, basil, olives, yogurt and drained cooked pasta. Toss until well-blended. Makes 5 or 6 servings.

Pasta Pilaf with Porcini Mushrooms

Dried porcini mushrooms provide a distinctive flavor. They are available in Italian markets or gourmet sections of supermarkets.

1 oz. dried porcini mushrooms
3 cups warm chicken broth
2 tablespoons margarine or butter
1 cup orzo
1 small onion, diced
1/2 cup grated Parmesan cheese
1 tablespoon chopped Italian parsley

Soak mushrooms in warm broth until soft, about 30 minutes. Slice soaked mushrooms crosswise; set aside. Line a medium strainer with a paper coffee filter. Strain soaking liquid through paper coffee filter or 2 layers of paper towels. Heat margarine or butter in a large skillet. Add uncooked orzo and onion. Stir and cook over medium heat about 2 minutes. Add half of strained chicken broth. Stir and cook until liquid is absorbed; repeat with remaining chicken broth. Add sliced mushrooms. Remove from heat. Add Parmesan cheese and sprinkle with chopped Italian parsley.
Makes 4 or 5 servings.

Sicilian Memories Caponata

*A flavorful combination of foods popular in
Mediterranean islands.*

8 oz. ziti or rigatoni (3 to 3-1/2 cups uncooked)
2 tablespoons olive oil
1 small eggplant, peeled, diced
1 small onion, chopped
1/2 lb. lean ground lamb
3 fresh Italian plum tomatoes, diced
1 garlic clove, crushed
2 tablespoons red-wine vinegar
1/4 teaspoon salt
1/8 teaspoon pepper
1/4 cup sliced ripe olives
Pine nuts

Cook pasta according to package directions; drain. Rinse
with hot water; drain and set aside. While pasta cooks, heat
olive oil in a large skillet. Add eggplant and onion; cook
10 minutes. Add lamb; cook and stir 3 to 5 minutes. Stir in
tomatoes, garlic, vinegar, salt and pepper. Simmer 1 or 2
minutes. Add olives. Spoon drained cooked pasta on a large
platter; pour eggplant mixture over top. Sprinkle with pine
nuts. Makes 5 or 6 servings.

Mandarin Shrimp & Noodles

Similar to sweet-sour shrimp, but noodles replace the traditional rice.

8 oz. medium noodles or fettucine
2 tablespoons vegetable oil
1 small red bell pepper, cut into small cubes
12 oz. medium uncooked shrimp, shelled
3 green onions, cut into 1-inch pieces
1 (11-oz.) can mandarin oranges in light syrup
1 tablespoon brown sugar
2 tablespoons soy sauce
2 tablespoons white-wine vinegar
1 garlic clove, crushed
1 tablespoon cornstarch
1 tablespoon toasted sesame seeds

Cook pasta according to package directions; drain. Rinse with hot water; drain and set aside in a large warm serving bowl. While pasta cooks, heat oil in a large skillet or wok. Add bell pepper, shrimp and green onions. Cook and stir 1 or 2 minutes. Drain oranges, reserving syrup. In a small bowl, combine orange syrup, brown sugar, soy sauce, vinegar, garlic and cornstarch. Stir into skillet; cook and stir until slightly thickened. Add drained mandarin oranges. Heat through, then spoon over drained cooked pasta. Sprinkle with toasted sesame seeds. Makes 5 or 6 servings.

Pronto Minestrone

Timesaver suggestions: use canned cut tomatoes, canned kidney beans and packaged shredded cabbage.

2 bacon slices, chopped
1 onion, chopped
2 carrots, peeled, finely chopped
1 (14-1/2-oz.) can cut peeled tomatoes
1 (15-oz.) can kidney beans, drained
2 zucchini, thinly sliced
2 cups shredded cabbage
6 cups beef broth or bouillon
1 cup small elbow macaroni or small shells (4 oz. uncooked)
1/2 teaspoon salt
1/8 teaspoon pepper
1 tablespoon chopped fresh basil
2 tablespoons chopped parsley

Cook bacon and onion in a 4-quart pan or Dutch oven. Add carrots, tomatoes, kidney beans, zucchini, cabbage, broth or bouillon, uncooked pasta, salt, pepper, basil and parsley. Cover; simmer 20 to 30 minutes or until vegetables are tender. Makes about 3-1/2 quarts.

Almost-Ready Dishes

Pasta is a nutritious and good-tasting "fast food" you can create in your own kitchen. If you're in the mood for prepared pasta, look for frozen or refrigerated items such as filled tortelloni, tortellini, agnolotti and ravioli. Also, you can enhance refrigerated or frozen fettucine or angel hair with ingredients you have on hand.

Other quick-and-easy combinations can be produced in your kitchen with dry pasta. Pronto Pesto Pasta features an almost instant pesto sauce whizzed in the food processor, then tossed with cooked angel hair or linguine. Or consider Shortcut Roquefort Fettucine. While the pasta cooks, heat the sauce ingredients and pour over drained cooked pasta; toss and serve.

Favorite Fettucine Alfredo

One of the most-famous pasta dishes.

8 oz. fettucine or linguine
1/2 cup butter
1 cup whipping cream or half and half
1/16 teaspoon ground nutmeg
1/4 teaspoon salt
1/8 teaspoon freshly ground pepper
2/3 cup grated Parmesan cheese

Cook pasta according to package directions; thoroughly drain but do not rinse. While pasta cooks, heat butter and cream in a large saucepan until blended. Stir in ground nutmeg, salt, pepper and drained cooked pasta. Add Parmesan cheese; toss until well-mixed. Serve immediately. Makes 4 or 5 servings.

Alfredo with a Lighter Touch

*Not as heavy or calorie-laden as the authentic recipe—
a welcome addition to a calorie-counter's menu.*

8 oz. fettucine or linguine
2 tablespoons margarine or butter, room temperature
3/4 cup half and half or evaporated skimmed milk
1/2 cup grated Parmesan cheese
1/4 teaspoon salt
1/8 teaspoon white pepper
1/8 teaspoon ground nutmeg

Cook pasta according to package directions; drain. Rinse with hot water; drain. Toss with margarine or butter in a large warm serving bowl. Add half of cream or evaporated milk; toss. Add half of Parmesan cheese; toss. Repeat with remaining cream or evaporated milk and Parmesan cheese, salt, pepper and nutmeg. Serve immediately.
Makes 4 or 5 servings.

Tortellini with Asparagus Sauce

Use fresh refrigerated pasta with asparagus soup for an impromptu meal.

1 (8-or 9-oz.) pkg. refrigerated cheese tortellini
1 (10-3/4-oz.) can condensed cream of asparagus soup,
    undiluted
1 (12-oz.) can evaporated skimmed milk
1 cup diced cooked ham or turkey
2 teaspoons Dijon-style mustard
1/8 teaspoon dried red-pepper flakes
1 teaspoon horseradish
Grated Parmesan cheese, if desired

Cook pasta according to package directions; drain. Rinse with hot water; drain and set aside in a large warm serving bowl. While pasta cooks, heat undiluted soup, evaporated milk, ham or turkey, mustard, red-pepper flakes and horseradish in a medium saucepan. Spoon over drained cooked tortellini. Sprinkle with Parmesan cheese, if desired. Makes about 4 servings.

Pronto Pesto Pasta

Take advantage of refrigerated pasta and sauces to produce a good meal within a few minutes.

1 (9-oz.) pkg. refrigerated ravioli with Italian sausage
2/3 cup refrigerated pesto sauce (6 oz.)
1 cup low-fat ricotta cheese (8 oz.)
1 small green or yellow bell pepper, diced
1 large tomato, diced

Cook pasta according to package directions; drain. Rinse with cold water; drain and set aside. In a serving large bowl, combine pesto, ricotta cheese, bell pepper and tomato. Add drained cooked pasta; toss until well-blended. Serve immediately or refrigerate several hours. Makes 4 servings.

Teriyaki Chicken & Noodles

A tasty, timesaving way to use cooked chicken or turkey.

8 oz. medium or wide noodles
2/3 cup bottled teriyaki sauce
1 garlic clove, crushed
1/2 teaspoon grated fresh ginger
1 tablespoon cornstarch
1 cup chicken broth or bouillon
1 (8-oz.) can sliced water chestnuts, drained
2 cups diced cooked chicken or turkey
Thinly sliced green onions

Cook pasta according to package directions; drain. Rinse with hot water; drain and set aside. While pasta cooks, combine teriyaki sauce, garlic, ginger, cornstarch, broth or bouillon, water chestnuts and chicken or turkey in a large skillet. Stir and heat until mixture begins to simmer and thicken. Add drained cooked pasta. Sprinkle with green onions. Makes 4 to 6 servings.

Gingered Shrimp with Linguine

Serve as soon as it is made or refrigerate for a couple of hours and enjoy it chilled.

8 oz. linguine or fettucine
2 tablespoons vegetable oil
1/2 cup half and half or whipping cream
2 green onions, thinly sliced
1 tablespoon grated fresh ginger
1 tablespoon lemon juice
1 tablespoon sesame oil
1/8 teaspoon salt
1/8 teaspoon seasoned pepper
8 oz. medium shrimp, shelled, cooked, halved
1 cup Chinese pea pods
1 tablespoon toasted sesame seeds

Cook pasta according to package directions; drain. Rinse with cold water; drain. Toss with vegetable oil in a large serving bowl. While pasta is cooking, combine half and half or whipping cream, green onions, ginger, lemon juice, sesame oil, salt, seasoned pepper and cooked shrimp in a medium bowl. Toss with drained cooked pasta and pea pods. Sprinkle with sesame seeds. Makes 4 to 6 servings.

Timesaver's Spaghetti

Start with a can or jar of prepared spaghetti sauce; enhance the flavor and texture with a small amount of ground turkey and zucchini.

8 oz. spaghetti or linguine
1 tablespoon vegetable oil
2 small zucchini, coarsely shredded
8 oz. ground turkey or chicken
1 tablespoon chopped fresh basil
1 (28-oz.) can or jar spaghetti sauce (without meat)
Grated Romano or Parmesan cheese, if desired

Cook pasta according to package directions; drain. Rinse with hot water; drain and set aside. While pasta cooks, heat oil in a large skillet. Add zucchini and ground turkey or chicken; stir and cook 5 to 6 minutes or until meat is done. Stir in basil and spaghetti sauce; heat until bubbly. Add drained cooked pasta. Sprinkle with Romano or Parmesan cheese, if desired. Makes 4 to 6 servings.

Quick Italian Toss

For an authentic Italian flavor, use freshly grated Parmigiana cheese.

8 oz. pasta twists or radiatore (about 2-1/2 to 3 cups uncooked)
1 cup ricotta cheese (8 oz.)
4 bacon slices, chopped
2 green onions, sliced
1 cup thawed frozen peas
1/4 teaspoon salt
1/8 teaspoon pepper
1/4 cup grated Parmesan cheese

Cook pasta according to package directions; drain. Rinse with hot water; drain. In a large serving bowl, toss ricotta with hot, cooked pasta. Meanwhile, cook chopped bacon in an 8-inch skillet. Add green onions, peas, salt and pepper. Cook and stir 2 or 3 minutes. Spoon over ricotta-coated pasta; toss until well-mixed. Top with Parmesan cheese. Makes 4 or 5 servings.

Tortellini Salad

Whip up this interesting main dish in a hurry—buy prepared tortellini at the deli or supermarket.

**1 lb. broccoflower, cut into bite-size pieces,
   cooked, drained, cooled**
1 small red or yellow bell pepper, cut in thin strips
2 green onions, thinly sliced
1 (9-oz.) pkg. fresh cheese-filled tortellini, cooked, drained
1/2 cup red-wine-vinegar salad dressing
20 to 24 extra-thin slices pepperoni, julienned (about 1 oz.)

In a large bowl, combine broccoflower, bell pepper, green onions and cooked tortellini. Add dressing; toss until well-blended. Sprinkle with pepperoni. Makes 4 or 5 servings.

Shortcut Roquefort Fettucine

Sauce is so quick and easy that it's ready before the pasta is done.

8 oz. fettucine or linguine
2 tablespoons margarine or butter
1 cup half and half or whipping cream
4 oz. Roquefort or blue cheese, crumbled
1/4 teaspoon salt
1/8 teaspoon pepper
2 tablespoons grated Parmesan cheese
1 tablespoon chopped parsley

Cook pasta according to package directions; drain. Rinse with hot water; drain and set aside in a large warm serving bowl. While pasta cooks, heat margarine or butter in a large skillet. Stir in half and half or cream, then blue cheese, salt and pepper. Heat and stir until mixture begins to bubble. Pour over drained cooked pasta; toss until coated. Sprinkle with Parmesan cheese and parsley. Makes 3 or 4 servings.

Basil-Pine-Nut Pasta

Slivers of cooked chicken or turkey added to this recipe make an excellent variation.

8 oz. angel hair or linguine
1 cup lightly packed basil leaves
1/3 cup pine nuts
1 garlic clove
1/4 teaspoon salt
1/8 teaspoon pepper
1/3 cup olive oil
1/4 cup grated Parmesan cheese

Cook pasta according to package directions; drain. Rinse with hot water; drain and set aside in a large warm serving bowl. While pasta cooks, process basil leaves, pine nuts, garlic, salt and pepper in a food processor until coarsely chopped. Gradually add olive oil while processor is running. Stir in Parmesan cheese. Toss with drained cooked pasta. Makes 4 or 5 servings.

Basil & Sun-Dried-Tomato Pasta

A quick-and-easy combination to impress impromptu guests.

8 oz. radiatore or bow ties (3-1/2 to 4 cups uncooked)
1/4 cup finely chopped sun-dried tomatoes in oil
1/4 cup finely chopped fresh basil
2 green onions, finely chopped
1 garlic clove, crushed
8 oz. Neufchâtel or cream cheese, room temperature
1/4 teaspoon seasoned salt
1/8 teaspoon pepper
1/3 cup milk
Fresh basil for garnish

Cook pasta according to package directions; drain. Rinse with hot water; drain and set aside. While pasta cooks, combine sun-dried tomatoes in a large serving bowl with basil, green onions, garlic, cheese, seasoned salt, pepper and milk. Add drained cooked pasta; toss until well-blended. Garnish with additional fresh basil.
Makes 4 or 5 servings.

Ham & Swiss Pasta

A creamy sauce full of the favorite ham and cheese combination.

8 oz. penne or medium shells (2-1/2 to 3 cups uncooked)
1/4 cup margarine or butter
1/4 cup all-purpose flour
2-3/4 cups milk
2 teaspoons prepared mustard
1/2 teaspoon horseradish
8 oz. shredded Swiss cheese (about 2-1/2 cups)
6 oz. cooked ham, cut into thin slivers (1-1/2 cups)
Chopped green onions, if desired

Cook pasta according to package directions; drain. Rinse with hot water; drain and set aside in a large warm serving bowl. In a medium saucepan, melt margarine or butter; stir in flour. Heat and stir until bubbly. Gradually stir in milk. Cook over medium heat, stirring constantly until thickened. Add mustard, horseradish, cheese and ham. Heat and stir until cheese melts. Pour over drained cooked pasta; toss until well-mixed. Sprinkle with chopped green onions, if desired. Makes 5 or 6 servings.

Double-Cheese-Basil Pasta with Pine Nuts

So easy to prepare and so wonderful to eat.

8 oz. corkscrews or rotelle (2-1/2 to 3 cups uncooked)
1 cup ricotta cheese (8 oz.)
1/2 cup grated Parmesan cheese
1 tablespoon finely chopped parsley
3 tablespoons finely chopped fresh basil
1/8 teaspoon black pepper
2 tablespoons vegetable oil or olive oil
1/2 teaspoon seasoned salt
2 tomatoes, finely chopped
1/4 cup toasted pine nuts

Cook pasta according to directions; drain. Rinse with hot water; drain and set aside in a large warm serving bowl. While pasta cooks, combine ricotta, Parmesan cheese, parsley, basil, pepper, oil, seasoned salt and chopped tomatoes in a medium bowl. Spoon over drained cooked pasta; toss until well-blended. Sprinkle with toasted pine nuts. Makes 4 to 6 servings.

Creamy Broccoli Angel Hair

If you keep these ingredients on hand, you can put this dish together within a few minutes.

8 oz. angel hair or thin spaghetti
1 tablespoon margarine or butter
2 green onions, chopped
1 (10-3/4-oz.) can condensed cream-of-broccoli soup
1/2 cup milk
1 (12-1/2-oz.) can chunk white chicken, drained
1/2 cup shredded Swiss or Emmenthaler cheese

Cook pasta according to package directions; drain. Rinse with hot water; drain. While pasta cooks, melt margarine or butter in a 2-1/2-quart microwaveable bowl on HIGH 20 to 30 seconds. Add green onions and microwave on HIGH 1 to 1-1/2 minutes. Stir in soup, milk and chicken. Microwave on HIGH 3-1/2 minutes. Stir in drained cooked pasta. Sprinkle top with cheese. Makes 4 to 6 servings.

Impromptu Pasta Toss

Add about a cup of cooked, shelled, medium shrimp for a more hearty main dish.

8 oz. radiatore or rotelle (3 to 3-1/4 cups uncooked)
1 (10-oz.) pkg. frozen broccoli cuts
1/4 cup olive oil
1 garlic clove, crushed
1/4 teaspoon crushed red-pepper flakes
1/4 cup grated Parmesan cheese

Cook pasta according to package directions; drain. Rinse with hot water; drain and set aside. Cook broccoli 6 to 7 minutes or until tender; drain. In a large warm serving bowl, combine drained cooked pasta, drained cooked broccoli, olive oil, garlic and red-pepper flakes; toss until well-blended. Sprinkle with Parmesan cheese. Makes 4 to 6 servings.

Picnics, Barbecues & Potlucks

Pasta is perfect for all kinds of casual outdoor get-togethers such as picnics, patio parties and barbecues. It blends well with typical outdoor foods such as burgers, hot dogs and barbecued chicken. A bowl of chilled Picnic Salad is a welcome addition to a neighborhood barbecue.

Picnic Salad

A hard-to-beat combination to go with burgers or steaks.

8 oz. medium shells or macaroni (2-1/2 cups uncooked)
1/2 cup mayonnaise
1/2 cup plain low-fat yogurt
1 tablespoon sugar
1 tablespoon vinegar
2 teaspoons prepared mustard
1/2 teaspoon salt
1/8 teaspoon pepper
1 cup cooked green peas
1 cup Gruyère or Swiss cheese cubes
2 green onions, chopped
1/4 cup chopped sweet pickles
1 hard-cooked egg, sliced, if desired

Cook pasta according to package directions; drain. Rinse with cold water; drain and cool. In a small bowl, combine mayonnaise, yogurt, sugar, vinegar, mustard, salt and pepper. In a large serving bowl, combine cooled cooked macaroni, green peas, cheese cubes, green onions and sweet pickles. Stir in mayonnaise mixture; toss to blend. Garnish with hard-cooked egg, if desired. Makes 4 to 6 servings.

Grilled Fish on Herbed Lemon Pasta

Try this popular combination the next time you barbecue.

8 oz. linguine or angel hair
1/4 cup margarine or butter
2 tablespoons all-purpose flour
2 cups half and half or milk
1 tablespoon chopped chives
1/4 cup lemon juice
1/4 teaspoon grated lemon peel
1 tablespoon chopped fresh dill
1 tablespoon chopped parsley
1/2 teaspoon salt
1/8 teaspoon pepper
1 lb. halibut or other steak fish, cut into 4 or 5 pieces

Cook pasta according to package directions; drain. Rinse
with hot water; drain and set aside in a large warm bowl.
While pasta cooks, heat margarine or butter in a large skillet.
Stir in flour, then half and half or milk and chives. Heat and
stir until thickened and bubbly. Add lemon juice, lemon
peel, dill, parsley, salt and pepper. Grill fish in a broiler or on
a barbecue. Arrange drained cooked pasta on
each dinner plate. Top with a serving of grilled
fish, then lemon-herb sauce.
Makes 4 or 5 servings.

Meal-in-a-Dish Linguine

An impressive addition to a potluck or picnic in the park.

8 oz. linguine or medium noodles
2 tablespoons margarine or butter
4 green onions, sliced
4 oz. mushrooms, (about 1-1/2 cups sliced)
2 tablespoons all-purpose flour
1/4 teaspoon salt
1/8 teaspoon pepper
1 cup half and half or whipping cream
1 cup cooked chopped broccoli
1 cup chopped cooked ham
1 cup shredded Cheddar or Monterey Jack cheese (4 oz.)

Cook pasta according to package directions; drain. Rinse
with hot water; drain and set aside. While pasta cooks, heat
margarine or butter in a large skillet. Add green onions and
mushrooms. Stir in flour, salt and pepper. Gradually stir in
half and half or cream; cook and stir until slightly thickened.
Add cooked broccoli and ham. Toss drained cooked pasta
with ham mixture. Serve immediately or spoon into a
2-1/2-quart shallow baking dish. Sprinkle with cheese.
Preheat oven to 375F (190C). Bake in preheated oven
30 to 35 minutes or until bubbly. Makes 5 or 6 servings.

Mozzarella Spaghetti Pie

It's easy to cut spaghetti pie into wedges if you let it stand five to ten minutes after it comes out of the oven.

8 oz. spaghetti
2 tablespoons vegetable oil
1/4 cup grated Parmesan cheese
1 egg, beaten slightly
4 oz. thinly sliced smoked Polish sausage (kielbasa)
1 (28-oz.) jar or can spaghetti sauce
1 cup shredded mozzarella cheese (4 oz.)
Additional Parmesan cheese, if desired

Cook spaghetti according to package directions; drain. Preheat oven to 375F (190C). In a large bowl, combine oil, Parmesan cheese and egg. Toss with drained cooked spaghetti. Lightly press half of spaghetti on bottom of a 10-inch shallow baking dish. Top with half of sliced sausage, then half of spaghetti sauce. Repeat with remaining spaghetti, sausage and sauce. Sprinkle with mozzarella cheese. Bake in preheated oven about 35 minutes or until bubbly. Cut into wedges. Serve with additional Parmesan cheese, if desired. Makes about 6 servings.

Grilled Chicken & Island Salsa on Noodles

Flavors of the tropics lend enchantment to grilled chicken.

8 oz. wide egg noodles
6 boneless skinless chicken-breast halves
2 tablespoons vegetable oil
1/4 teaspoon salt
2 tablespoons finely chopped red onion
1 teaspoon grated fresh ginger
1 fresh California green chili, seeded, chopped
1 papaya, peeled, seeded, chopped
1 (8-oz.) can crushed pineapple, drained
2 tablespoons flaked coconut

Cook pasta according to package directions; drain. Rinse with hot water; drain and set aside on a warm platter. While pasta cooks, brush chicken with oil. Sprinkle with salt. Grill 5 minutes. Brush with oil; turn and grill other side 4 to 6 minutes. In a small bowl, combine red onion, ginger, green chili, papaya and pineapple. Arrange grilled chicken breasts on drained cooked noodles. Spoon salsa over chicken. Top with coconut. Makes 6 servings.

Creamy Spinach-Topped Turkey Bake

Save lots of preparation time by buying shredded mozzarella cheese, prepared marinara sauce and frozen spinach in cream sauce.

8 oz. lasagne noodles
1 tablespoon vegetable oil
8 oz. ground turkey
1 (30-oz.) jar marinara sauce
2 tablespoons dry white wine
1 (9-1/2-oz.) pkg. thawed frozen creamed spinach
1 egg, beaten slightly
1/8 teaspoon ground nutmeg
2 cups shredded mozzarella cheese (8 oz.)
1/4 cup grated Romano or Parmesan cheese

Cook pasta according to package directions; drain. Rinse with cold water; drain and set aside. While pasta cooks, heat oil in a large skillet. Add ground turkey. Cook, stirring to break up turkey, 2 or 3 minutes. Stir in marinara sauce and wine; set aside. Preheat oven to 350F (175C). In a medium bowl, combine spinach, egg and nutmeg. Using half of each mixture, arrange alternate layers of marinara sauce with turkey, shredded mozzarella, drained cooked lasagne noodles and spinach-egg mixture in a 13" x 9" baking dish. Repeat layers. Top with Romano or Parmesan cheese. Bake in preheated oven 25 to 30 minutes or until bubbly.
Makes about 8 servings.

Pizza-Pasta Burgers

Flavors borrowed from your favorite pizzas, then served over a bed of noodles.

8 oz. medium or fine noodles
1-1/2 lbs. lean ground beef
2 tablespoons grated Parmesan cheese
2 tablespoons finely chopped onion
1/4 teaspoon salt
1/8 teaspoon pepper
2 (8-oz.) cans tomato sauce
1 teaspoon chopped fresh oregano
1 garlic clove, crushed
1 cup shredded mozzarella cheese (4 oz.)
2 tablespoons sliced ripe olives, if desired

Cook pasta according to package directions; drain. Rinse with hot water; drain and set aside in a large warm bowl. While pasta cooks, combine meat with Parmesan cheese, onion, salt and pepper in a large bowl. Form mixture into 6 patties. Broil until they reach desired doneness. In a small saucepan, heat tomato sauce, oregano and garlic. Spoon drained cooked noodles onto a large platter. Arrange cooked burgers on top. Spoon heated tomato mixture over all. Sprinkle with cheese, then olives, if desired.
Makes 6 servings.

Roasted Red-Pepper & Corn Surprise

To roast a pepper, place in broiler or on barbecue grill until skin is dark and blistered. Turn pepper over and repeat broiling.

8 oz. penne or elbow macaroni (about 2-1/2 cups uncooked)
2 ears fresh corn
1 red bell pepper, roasted, peeled, seeded, coarsely chopped
1 garlic clove, crushed
2 green onions, cut into quarters
1/4 teaspoon salt
1/8 teaspoon pepper
1/2 cup crumbled goat cheese (about 3 oz.)

Cook pasta according to package directions; drain. Rinse with hot water; drain and set aside in a large warm serving bowl. While pasta cooks, remove husks and silk from corn. Cut corn off cob. In a blender or food processor, combine corn, roasted pepper, garlic, green onions, salt and pepper. Process until chopped but not puréed. Toss with drained cooked pasta. Sprinkle with crumbled goat cheese. Serve as main dish or as accompaniment to grilled meat.
Makes 4 or 5 servings.

Pepperoni-Cheese Lasagne

Although the name of this dish will puzzle your friends, they will love the flavor combination.

8 oz. lasagne noodles (9 uncooked)
1 (29-oz.) can tomato sauce
1/2 teaspoon dried-leaf oregano
1 cup ricotta cheese (8 oz.)
1 cup thinly sliced mushrooms
1 (6-oz.) pkg. mozzarella cheese, sliced
3-1/2 oz. thinly sliced pepperoni, halved (55 to 60 slices)
1/4 cup grated Parmesan cheese

Cook lasagne noodles according to package directions; drain. Rinse with cold water; drain and set aside. While lasagne cooks, combine tomato sauce and oregano in a medium bowl. In a 13" x 9" baking pan, arrange alternate layers of one-third of drained cooked lasagne noodles, ricotta cheese, tomato sauce, sliced mushrooms, mozzarella cheese and pepperoni. Repeat layering 2 more times. Preheat oven to 350F (175C). Sprinkle Parmesan cheese over all. Bake in preheated oven 35 to 40 minutes.
Makes 6 to 8 servings.

Occidental Noodles

Use as a vegetarian main dish or serve with grilled chicken breast.

8 oz. vermicelli or fine noodles (about 4 cups uncooked)
1 tablespoon vegetable oil
1 (16-oz.) pkg. Oriental-blend frozen vegetables
1 garlic clove, crushed
1/4 cup soy sauce
1/4 cup white wine
1 teaspoon grated fresh ginger
3/4 cup orange juice
1 tablespoon cornstarch
1 tablespoon water
1 cup firm tofu, cut in 1/2-inch cubes (6 oz.)
1/2 cup toasted almonds or cashews

Cook pasta according to package directions; drain. Rinse with hot water; drain and set aside. In a large skillet or wok, heat oil. Add frozen vegetables and garlic. Heat and stir 2 or 3 minutes. Stir in soy sauce, white wine, ginger and orange juice. Dissolve cornstarch in water; add to skillet. Stir and cook about 1 minute. Cover and cook 3 or 4 minutes or until vegetables are tender. Stir in tofu, then drained cooked pasta. Top with almonds or cashews.
Makes 4 to 6 servings.

Celebrations & Parties

So you decided to have a party! Now to select foods with universal appeal—something all your friends will enjoy. Did you know that everyone loves pasta? And you can make unbelievable show-off combinations ranging from down-home dishes to a cornucopia of ethnic and regional specialties.

You might start dinner with an appetizer of Angel Hair with Brie & Crabmeat. Or impress your guests with a buffet featuring Tarragon Turkey Platter. This easy-to-make main dish features turkey breast and your favorite vegetables in a creamy wine sauce on a base of linguine.

Angel Hair with Brie & Crabmeat

Cooked, shelled small shrimp make an excellent substitute if crabmeat is not readily available.

8 oz. angel hair or spaghettini
8 oz. Brie cheese, diced
1/2 cup half and half or whipping cream
2 tablespoons chopped watercress
6 to 8 oz. cooked crabmeat, flaked
Lemon slices

Cook pasta according to package directions; drain well. Immediately toss with diced Brie, half and half or cream and watercress. Divide into individual servings. Top each with crabmeat. Garnish with lemon slices. Makes 6 appetizers or 4 main-dish servings.

Party-Time Straw & Hay Fettucine

This popular, classic combination of spinach pasta with its natural-colored cousin has spawned many variations.

8 oz. spinach fettucine
8 oz. regular fettucine
1/4 cup butter or margarine
1 onion, chopped
1 garlic clove, crushed
2 tablespoons chopped fresh basil
1/2 teaspoon salt
1/8 teaspoon pepper
1/4 cup dry white wine
2 cups half and half
8 oz. boiled ham or 4 oz. prosciutto, cut into thin strips
1 (10-oz.) pkg. thawed frozen peas
1 cup sliced mushrooms
1 cup grated Parmesan cheese

Preheat oven to 375F (190C). Cook both pastas in the same pot according to package directions; drain and set aside. Do not rinse. While pasta cooks, heat butter or margarine in a large skillet. Add onion and garlic; cook 3 to 5 minutes or until onion softens. Stir in basil, salt, pepper, wine, half and half, then ham or prosciutto, peas and mushrooms. Simmer 2 minutes. Stir drained cooked pasta and half of Parmesan cheese into ham mixture. Spoon into a 13" x 9" baking dish. Sprinkle with remaining Parmesan cheese. Bake 15 minutes or until bubbly. Makes 10 to 12 servings.

Tarragon Turkey Platter

There are many frozen-vegetable mixtures. We chose the combination of broccoli, carrots and cauliflower for this dish.

8 oz. linguine or spaghetti
2 tablespoons margarine or butter
6 to 8 boneless turkey-breast slices (1 to 1-1/4 lbs.)
1/4 cup all-purpose flour
1 (16-oz.) pkg. frozen broccoli, carrots and cauliflower
2 teaspoons chopped fresh tarragon
1/2 teaspoon salt
1/8 teaspoon pepper
2 tablespoons dry white wine
1 cup chicken broth or bouillon
1 cup dairy sour cream
Chopped chives, if desired

Cook pasta according to package directions; drain. Rinse with hot water; drain and set aside. While pasta cooks, heat margarine or butter in a large skillet. Coat slices of turkey with flour. Lightly brown on both sides. Add frozen vegetables, tarragon, salt, pepper, wine and chicken broth to skillet. Cover; simmer about 12 minutes or until vegetables are tender. Stir in sour cream. Spoon over drained cooked pasta on a large platter. Sprinkle with chopped chives, if desired. Makes 6 servings.

Rolled Florentine Lasagne

Put these ingredients together the day before a party or potluck, then refrigerate until it's time to bake.

8 oz. lasagne noodles (9 or 10 uncooked)
8 oz. lean ground beef
1 small onion, chopped
1 garlic clove, crushed
1 (16-oz.) can tomato sauce
1 (16-oz.) can chopped tomatoes in juice
1 teaspoon chopped fresh oregano
2 teaspoons chopped fresh basil
1/4 teaspoon salt
1/8 teaspoon pepper
1 egg, beaten slightly
2 cups small-curd cottage cheese
1 tablespoon chopped parsley
2 tablespoons fine dry bread crumbs
1/2 cup grated Parmesan cheese
1 (10-oz.) pkg. thawed frozen chopped spinach, well-drained

Cook lasagne noodles according to package directions; drain. Rinse with hot water; drain and set aside. While pasta cooks, brown ground beef and onion in a large skillet. Add garlic, tomato sauce, chopped tomatoes, oregano, basil, salt and pepper; simmer 5 minutes. Spoon one-third of meat mixture in the bottom of a 13" x 9" baking pan. In a small bowl, combine egg, cottage cheese, parsley, bread crumbs, half of Parmesan cheese and well-drained spinach. Spread equal amounts of egg mixture on each drained cooked lasagne noodle; roll up. Preheat oven to 350F (175C). Place rolls on their sides, on top of cooked meat in pan. Spoon remaining two-thirds of meat mixture over all. Sprinkle with remaining Parmesan cheese. Bake in preheated oven 25 to 30 minutes or until bubbly. Makes 10 servings.

Pork-Tenderloin & Mushroom Special

Wrap whole pork tenderloin in plastic or freezer wrap; then partially freeze for easier cutting and more uniform slices.

8 oz. pasta nuggets or twists (about 3 cups uncooked)
12 oz. to 1 lb. pork tenderloin
1 tablespoon vegetable oil
1 tablespoon cornstarch
1-1/2 cups chicken broth or bouillon
1 leek, thinly sliced
1/4 teaspoon salt
1/8 teaspoon pepper
1 cup sliced mushrooms
1 tablespoon chopped fresh dill weed
1 cup plain low-fat yogurt
Chopped dill for garnish

Cook pasta according to package directions; drain. Rinse with hot water; drain and set aside in a large warm serving bowl. With a sharp knife, cut tenderloin into 1/4-inch crosswise slices. Heat oil in a large skillet. Lightly brown slices of tenderloin. In a small bowl, combine cornstarch and broth or bouillon. Add to skillet with leek, salt, pepper, mushrooms and dill. Cook and stir until bubbly and thickened. Add yogurt. Spoon over drained cooked pasta. Sprinkle with extra chopped dill. Makes 5 to 7 servings.

Jumbo Stuffed Shells

Mascarpone is available in cheese shops and gourmet cheese sections of supermarkets. If not available, whip an equal amount of cream cheese and add sugar to taste.

12 jumbo pasta shells (about 3-1/2 oz. uncooked)
1 cup mascarpone
4 to 6 oz. blue cheese or Gorgonzola
1 tablespoon chopped chives
1/4 cup margarine or butter
2 large onions, thinly sliced
1 (14-1/2-oz.) can cut Italian-style tomatoes (with garlic, oregano and basil)

Cook large shells according to package directions; drain. Rinse with hot water and set aside. While pasta cooks, combine mascarpone in a small bowl with blue cheese or Gorgonzola and chives. Fill drained cooked shells with cheese mixture. In a large skillet, heat margarine or butter. Add onions; stir and sauté over low heat until soft and golden. Stir in tomatoes; simmer 2 or 3 minutes. Carefully add filled shells to skillet with sauce. Cover; cook over very low heat 3 to 5 minutes or until shells are hot.
Makes 12 jumbo shells.

Holiday Fettucine

For a variety in color combinations, substitute yellow or orange peppers for the red ones.

8 oz. spinach fettucine or noodles
2 tablespoons margarine or butter
1 garlic clove, crushed
2 red bell peppers, seeded, chopped
1 green or red jalapeño pepper, seeded, finely chopped
1 red onion, chopped
1/4 teaspoon salt
2 tablespoons tomato paste
1/4 cup chicken broth
2 tablespoons chopped pistachios

Cook pasta according to package directions; drain. Rinse with hot water; drain and set aside in a large warm serving bowl. While pasta cooks, melt margarine or butter in a large skillet. Add garlic, bell peppers, jalapeño and onion; sauté 3 to 5 minutes. Stir in salt, tomato paste and broth. Purée pepper mixture in a food processor or blender. Pour over cooked drained pasta; toss until well-blended. Top with pistachios. Makes 4 or 5 servings.

Shortcut Manicotti

Use prepared spaghetti sauce or chopped canned tomatoes to save time.

10 manicotti shells
1-1/2 cups ricotta cheese (12 oz.)
1 cup shredded Monterey Jack cheese (4 oz.)
2 tablespoons finely chopped parsley
1 tablespoon finely chopped fresh basil
4 oz. chopped prosciutto (about 1 cup)
2 eggs, beaten
1 (26-oz.) jar or can tomato and basil pasta sauce
1/4 cup grated Parmesan cheese

Cook manicotti shells according to package directions; drain. Rinse with cold water; drain and set aside. While pasta cooks, combine ricotta with Monterey Jack cheese. Stir in parsley, basil, prosciutto and beaten eggs. Preheat oven to 375F (190C). Fill drained cooked manicotti shells with cheese mixture. Spoon about one-fourth of pasta sauce in the bottom of a 13" x 9" baking dish. Arrange a single layer of filled shells on pasta sauce. Spoon remaining sauce around and over tops of stuffed manicotti. Sprinkle with Parmesan cheese. Bake in preheated oven 30 minutes or until bubbly. Makes 10 filled manicotti shells.

New-Style Jambalaya

The same traditional seasonings as the classic dish, but featuring turkey instead of chicken.

2 tablespoons vegetable oil
3/4 to 1 lb. boneless skinless turkey or chicken breast, cubed
1 onion, finely chopped
1 green or red bell pepper, finely chopped
1/2 cup finely chopped celery
1 garlic clove, crushed
1 (16-oz.) can diced peeled tomatoes
1/2 teaspoon dried Italian seasoning
1/2 teaspoon chili powder
1/2 teaspoon salt
8 oz. kielbasa or light smoked turkey, beef and pork
  sausage, diced
2 cups chicken broth or bouillon
1 cup uncooked orzo

Heat oil in a 4-quart Dutch oven. Lightly brown turkey or chicken. Add onion, bell pepper, celery, garlic, tomatoes, Italian seasoning, chili powder, salt, smoked sausage, broth or bouillon and uncooked orzo. Cover and cook over medium heat 20 to 30 minutes or until pasta is done. Makes 6 to 8 servings.

Pasta with Four Cheeses

Known as Quattro Formaggi *at many well-known pasta restaurants. Vary the combination of cheeses to include your favorite kinds.*

8 oz. fettucine or medium noodles
2 tablespoons margarine or butter
2 tablespoons all-purpose flour
1/2 cup chicken broth
1 cup half and half
1/8 teaspoon ground nutmeg
1/2 cup shredded Gruyère or Swiss cheese
1/2 cup crumbled goat cheese
1/4 cup crumbled Gorgonzola cheese
1/2 cup grated Parmesan cheese

Cook pasta according to package directions; drain. Rinse with hot water; drain and set aside in a large warm serving bowl. While pasta cooks, melt margarine or butter in a large skillet; stir in flour. Add broth, half and half and nutmeg. Cook and stir over medium heat until thickened. Stir in Gruyère or Swiss cheese. Spoon sauce over drained cooked pasta; toss until well-blended. Sprinkle with goat cheese and Gorgonzola. Toss, then top with Parmesan cheese.
Makes 4 or 5 servings.

Mini Pork Pouches

For best results, use very lean ground pork. If not available, purchase lean, uncooked cutlets or chops and chop finely in your food processor.

1 lb. lean ground pork
1/4 cup low-sodium soy sauce
1 tablespoon finely chopped chives
1 tablespoon grated fresh ginger
1 tablespoon honey
1 garlic clove, crushed
32 round won-ton skins (about 3-1/2-inch diameter)

Dip:
1 tablespoon dry mustard
2 tablespoons low-sodium soy sauce
2 tablespoons rice-wine vinegar
1 teaspoon sesame oil

In a medium bowl, combine ground pork, soy sauce, chives, ginger, honey and garlic. Spoon about 1 tablespoon mixture into center of each won-ton skin. Pleat skin around filling to make a little pouch, leaving center of top open. Arrange on a rack in a pan over boiling water. Cover pan; steam 8 to 10 minutes. Dip pouches into sauce or spoon sauce over top. Makes 32 pouches.

Dip:
In a small bowl, gradually add dry mustard to soy sauce. Stir in vinegar and sesame oil.

Smoked-Albacore Pasta

Double this recipe for a party or impromptu get-together.

8 oz. rigatoni or mostaccioli (about 3-1/2 cups uncooked)
2 tablespoons vegetable oil
1 small onion, chopped
4 fresh Italian tomatoes, chopped
1/3 cup red wine
1/4 teaspoon salt
1/8 teaspoon pepper
1/2 cup half and half
8 oz. smoked albacore or other smoked fish

Cook pasta according to package directions; drain. Rinse with hot water; drain and set aside. While pasta cooks, heat oil in a 10-inch skillet. Add onion, tomatoes, wine, salt and pepper. Cover; simmer 5 minutes. Stir in half and half and drained cooked pasta; heat until bubbly. Remove any bones or skin from smoked fish. Cut into bite-size pieces. Add to pasta and sauce. Heat 2 minutes. Makes 4 to 6 servings.

Index